Who's In Charge Here?

Who's In Charge Here?

Overcoming Power Struggles With Your Kids

Dr. Bob Barnes

ZONDERVAN™

GRAND RAPIDS, MICHIGAN 49530 USA

ZONDERVAN™

Who's In Charge Here?
Copyright © 1990 by Robert G. Barnes
First Zondervan edition, 1997

Requests for information should be addressed to:

Zondervan, *Grand Rapids, Michigan 49530*

Library of Congress Cataloging-in-Publication Data

Barnes, Robert G.
    Who's in charge here? : overcoming power struggles with your kids / Bob
Barnes.
       p. cm.
    Originally published: Dallas : Word Pub., c 1990.
    ISBN 0-310-21743-1 (pbk.)
    1. Discipline of children—United States. 2. Parents and children—United
States. 3. Parenting—United States—Religious aspects—Christianity. I. Title.
[HQ770.4.B38 1997]
649'.64—dc21   97-3343
                                                          CIP

Verses marked (KJV) are from The King James Version of the Bible.

Scripture quotations marked (NKJV) in this publication are from *The New King James
Bible Version.* Copyright © 1979, 1980, 1982, Thomas Nelson, Inc.

Verses marked (TLB) are taken from *The Living Bible,* © 1971. Used by permission of
Tyndale House Publishers, Inc., Wheaton, IL 60189. All rights reserved.

CONTENTS

CONTENTS

ACKNOWLEDGMENT

To acknowledge the help of others is, in and of itself, a discipline. Most of us need help in the area of disciplining ourselves to thank those around us who have found a way to make positive contributions to our lives. German pragmatist that I am, I often forget that God has sent many special encouragers into my life. I, more than most, need to discipline myself to say thanks.

As I was beginning this book, a friend found out that I had written my previous books in longhand. He immediately purchased new computers for Sheridan House Family Ministries and my home. I am very grateful to Gary and Cecilia Peters for this generous contribution.

To get me away from the office so that I could write, Vic and Sally Miranda, as well as Dan and Julie Smith, made their cabins available to my family. This vote of confidence was a great encouragement.

I will always be grateful for the privilege of working at Sheridan House Family Ministries. The board of directors and staff have worked hard to help make the time necessary for me to write and for Rosemary and me to conduct seminars. We are both thankful for the way this Sheridan House family has pushed us to new challenges.

The disciplined life of my dad continues to stand as an example to me. He set boundaries for his family that were easily discernible, and then he lived within them himself. His example of personal discipline has been a model for me.

Anyone who has read this book will quickly find that my wife, Rosemary, is much more than a spouse. She is the best friend I have and acts as if her ideas were mine to begin with. I shall remain eternally grateful for her influence in my life. It was Rosemary who led me to Christ, my Foundation for life.

INTRODUCTION

Today's family has become a vacuum for leadership. No one seems to be in charge of anything but themselves. Even leadership of one's self has shown us to be a people controlled by feelings. People do things because they feel like it rather than because it is the right thing to do.

No one seems to be in charge in today's homes, and that's because few want the responsibility. We want the privileges that come with being a part of a family unit, but the responsibilities seem too difficult.

When my son Robey was five years old, he got very excited about purchasing a new backpack. He figured that since it was time to enter kindergarten he would need a backpack to carry all his things to school.

For a long time Robey had his eye on a very special backpack. It had a camouflage design on it and looked more like something one would wear into a swamp rather than to school. But this is what he wanted.

A week before school we purchased his backpack together, and he wore it out the door of the department store. A strange thing happened when the first day of school arrived, however. Robey put his lunch in the new backpack, and when we started out the door for school, he handed it to me. "Would you carry it for me, Daddy?" he asked me.

I couldn't believe it. After all the begging he went through to get it, now Robey didn't want to wear the new backpack.

"Robey," I responded, "I thought you wanted this backpack?"

"I do, Daddy," Robey said, "I just don't want to have to carry it."

It was a classic response. My son wanted the privilege of having something, but he didn't want the responsibility of carrying it.

This is exactly the case where discipline in the home is concerned. Parent and child often spend a lifetime battling over who is to carry the responsibility for decisions and consequences. Parents tell their children to do something, and when their children don't do it, the parents do little more than get frustrated. The little more that they actually do is to take care of the task themselves.

"Son, the cleaning of your closet will be your responsibility from now on," a mother might announce to her child. Then the struggle begins.

Parent and child battle over who is really in charge of cleaning that closet. Lectures, threats, and various punishments are used. The parent wants the child to be responsible enough to do the chore assigned without constantly having to be reminded. The child doesn't particularly want that responsibility.

This power struggle is often terminated when the parent gives in. Rather than accepting the responsibility for teaching the child to clean the closet, the parent does it herself. This keeps the peace, keeps the child friends with the parent, but ultimately, it keeps the child from learning the much needed lesson for life: the discipline of accepting responsibility.

This book is about how to establish discipline and responsibility in the home in such a way that parent and child will be able to like each other. It is my intention to help parents get out of the power struggle and the game of threats. I want to help them stop yelling and screaming and making themselves the enemy. These are things any parent can do, but it means using a plan that helps children know that it is their job to carry certain responsibilities in life.

This book will help you teach your child how to be responsible for his own behavior and thus his own future.

PART I

Responsibility:
Who's in Charge?

1

Childhood: The Building Block for Adulthood

BILL WALKED out of his boss's office knowing his days with this company were numbered. It was the same old problem. He had been given an assignment, and once again he had missed the deadline.

Several months ago, Bill had been assigned the task of completing an inventory in one of his company's warehouses. His boss, George, told him the job needed to be completed in thirty days. The deadline arrived and passed. Bill had not been able to buckle down and complete the assignment, so he was given an extension. Three extensions later, Bill was still not completely finished.

There was a time when Bill was given jobs of more significance. In fact, years ago, Bill was actually George's boss. That did not last long, however. A basic difference between Bill and George caused the tables to turn.

George had an ability to go out on his own and complete his assigned tasks. He was a self-starter and didn't need anyone looking over his shoulder. He was successful because he was able to finish his work long before it was due. As a result, he quickly rose through the company ranks.

Bill, on the other hand, needed close supervision. He started his jobs with great enthusiasm but always seemed to lose steam. With no discipline to organize his time, he would procrastinate until the last minute. Bill's difficulties stemmed from a childhood deficiency. That deficiency— lack of discipline—had caused him to lose responsibilities within the company and to be passed over for promotions as George advanced. Now Bill's lack of discipline was about to cost him his job.

Linda, a thirty-four-year-old mother of two little boys, had a similar problem with self-discipline. She had been married for eleven years, and as these years had passed, so too had her attractive figure. Linda could not stay out of the cookies and pastries. This was not a new problem for Linda; she had always battled to keep her weight down. Through high school and college she had been able to win this battle and, in the process, the affections of Ed.

Shortly after graduation from college, Linda and Ed were married. At first her weight only slipped a little. Then came her first pregnancy. Linda never regained her figure after the baby was born. And her second pregnancy left her even larger—forty-five pounds over her wedding weight. By her second child's sixth birthday, Linda was sixty-two pounds over the weight she had been eleven years before—and still climbing.

If you asked Linda why she didn't do something about her weight, you would hear an amazing list of excuses.

"I would lose weight if Ed didn't nag me about it."

"I would stay on my diet if Ed would only encourage me."

"How can anyone with children in the house ever lose weight? Their constant snacks and cookies get me down."

The one consistent thread in Linda's excuses is her attempt to blame her weight gain on everyone else. The reality of Linda's apparent lack of control comes from the same childhood deficiency that Bill suffers from.

Jack has ruined his life with a different problem. At age forty, Jack has come to believe that he is just not a one-woman man. He loves his wife, Elizabeth, and both of them are physically attractive individuals. Jack's statement to a counselor was, "I don't know what happens to me. Elizabeth is a wonderful woman. Every time I see an opportunity to be with another woman, however, I just can't resist. I guess I'm just one of those guys who is not a one-woman man."

The fact that Jack "couldn't resist" the advances of other women is an immaturity that has plagued him throughout the eight years of his marriage. As a last resort, this man went to see a counselor. This effort, itself, was only motivated by the fact that Elizabeth had also gone to see someone—a lawyer.

Jack suffered from many problems. However, one of these was the same kind of childhood deficiency that affected Bill and Linda.

Finally, let's look at the story of Steve and Donna. They are both college graduates and both earn excellent incomes. Financially speaking, this couple should have been on top of the world with no worries at all.

Unfortunately the opposite was the case. Instead of being on top of the world financially, they had dug themselves into a deep pit and were over their heads with debt.

It began the week Steve got his first paycheck from the accounting firm that hired him after graduation. He didn't have the money for the down payment on the BMW he bought that week, so he borrowed it.

Donna followed a similar pattern of spending after graduation, buying clothing at a rate substantially beyond her earrings. She justified her uncontrolled spending as necessary because she was preparing for her new job, as well as her upcoming wedding to Steve.

This couple married and found lending institutions more than eager to help them live beyond their earnings. Steve and Donna accumulated a thick stack of credit cards that allowed them to continue an unrestrained wave of purchases. If they wanted it, they bought it—or charged it, we should say. It mattered little, until they began to receive the daily letters and phone calls from their anxious lenders. Steve and Donna had destroyed their credit, their credibility, and almost their marriage. All this because they could not say no to their wants.

How does this happen to two educated individuals? It happens the same way it happened to Bill, Linda, and Jack—it happens because as children they did not learn how to say no to their desires, or to the temptations that we all face on a daily basis. Their lack of childhood training is the key to their problems as adults.

Children Need Basic Training, Too

Many young men go through an eight-week instructional period called Basic Training as they enter the military. It is a time of intense emotional, mental, and physical training. It is not, as some may think, a time to simply humiliate new soldiers, to teach them how to do push-ups, or become good rope climbers. Nor is it a time to teach soldiers how to cower beneath the screams of a particular drill instructor. Rather, the purpose for the eight weeks of Basic Training is to make the new soldiers self-disciplined individuals so they will be able to perform effectively in a combat situation.

By putting recruits through this organized system of discipline, it is hoped they will learn to avoid mistakes, that they will be able to function to their full potential, and that they will be able to survive difficult situations.

Likewise, childhood basic training helps children grow into responsible adults who function to their full potential—and survive the varied challenges hurled at them in everyday life.

The five people in the examples at the beginning of this chapter either missed or did not grasp this form of childhood basic training. They are not unique. Many adults in today's world grew up in homes that did not have a plan for training or discipline. Their parents felt that boundaries would only stifle the children's creativity. Their homes functioned with no plan, no training, no discipline—in reality, no parenting.

The word discipline does not denote a negative form of action. A disciplinary plan is a system that establishes boundaries for a child and allows the child to make decisions concerning those boundaries. The parent enforces the boundaries while loving the child. The child is taught to accept the responsibility, consequences, and rewards for his behavior.

Responsibility is the key. The child must be placed in a position of being responsible for his behavior. The parent must be in the position of loving the child while upholding the behavioral boundaries.

Perhaps the people in the beginning of this chapter had never been given responsibility for their lives and behavior as children. Consequently, they entered adulthood with an immature understanding of personal discipline.

Remember overweight Linda? She said, "I'm not responsible for this obesity. It's Ed's fault because he doesn't encourage me, and it's the children's fault because they have snacks." She still functioned as a child as far as accepting responsibility was concerned. She had no personal discipline!

Summary

When discipline is not a basic part of a child's training, it will affect their future adult behavior.

1. Lack of discipline can impact a person's professional or vocational potential.

2. Lack of discipline can impact a person's physical well-being and self-esteem.

3. Lack of discipline can impact a person's ability to resist temptation.

4. Lack of discipline can affect the stewardship of a person's possessions.

Discipline, or the lack of it, will affect every area of a person's life.

2

Why Is Discipline Necessary?

WHY IS DISCIPLINE necessary? This is a question on the hearts of all parents when they bring that bundle of joy home from the hospital. *Look how sweet she looks,* I remember thinking. *She couldn't have a disobedient bone in her body.*

But training of the child must start at a very early age. And it's the *purpose* of this training that is so significant for all parents to understand. A plan of training and discipline is not to teach the child how to avoid ripping pages out of your favorite book. It's not even done so that the youngster will be obedient. A consistent plan of training is necessary so that parent and child can *understand* and *love* each other. It is part of the child's development and an important part of becoming a fully functioning adult. Discipline is necessary for each person to reach his or her full potential.

But what about that cute toddler? How did he go from sweet innocence to rebellion? How did he learn to be disobedient? I was in graduate school during those years when we were taught that children are initially good, that they are not born disobedient, and that their environment is to blame for turning them into disobedient brats. Surely the academic scholars who propagated that thought were certainly never parents!

Children are born to be just like the rest of us: *self*-centered. They want all of society to revolve around them. So, besides loving their children, parents have the task of molding them to fit into society. The two roles must go hand in hand—the child needs to grow up in an environment of love so that he feels valuable to himself and in an environment of boundaries so that he becomes valuable to society.

The First Boundary: No!

At a very early age a healthy child begins to test these boundaries—not because his environment has polluted him, but because he is imperfect and self-centered like everyone else.

As Torrey, our first child, began to crawl and walk around the house, we had to make some basic decisions. How should we, as parents, set up the boundaries in her world? It was my plan to move everything in the house that was within her grasp.

My wife, Rosemary, knew that this would be impossible. She suggested that we remove only some things. Rosemary's idea was to remove some of the books from the lower shelves of the bookcases and to replace them with some of Torrey's toys. The other lower shelves would still have books, and we would teach Torrey that they were off-limits to her.

"After all, Bob, Torrey is going to need to learn the word *no*," Rosemary told me.

I, on the other hand, felt that fourteen months was much too early for a child to learn the word *no*. "Rosemary, it's not that Torrey will be disobedient; she's too young to be rebellious. If she touches something that she's not supposed to, it's our fault. We should have removed it from her environment."

Child expert that I was, my patient wife, with eight years of experience as a public schoolteacher, gave in to my plan. We removed all the books from three feet on down, as well as anything else that might require us to use the word *no!* With that plan of action, I felt certain little Torrey would never learn to be a rebellious child.

Each morning our family meets in the living room after breakfast. We have a time of family devotions while Rosemary and I drink a cup of coffee. When she was younger, Torrey, holding her bottle of juice, always sat on the floor or in one of our laps.

She was permitted to set the juice bottle down many places; but one place was out of bounds. The special coffee table in front of the couch was forbidden territory. I never put my coffee cup there, and she had been taught by her mother not to put her bottle there, either. I might add that she had learned this rule quite well. I had never seen her even try to put her bottle on that forbidden table.

One morning we were all in the living room, and I had just finished reading the family devotions. Rosemary left the room to get us a refill of coffee. As if on cue, fourteen-month-old Torrey got up with her bottle and waddled over to the coffee table.

Somewhat surprised, I watched my little girl walk deliberately toward the forbidden territory. "Please don't put your bottle on the table, Torrey," I tried. Then as she got to the table, I said once more with authority, "Torrey, no. Don't do that, honey." As long as I live, I will never forget the look on her face.

Torrey stopped, lifted the bottle, turned to look at me, and with a big, mischievous smile, slammed the bottle down on the table as hard as she could.

Her little face expressed volumes. It was as if she said to me, "Says who, Daddy? I know Mommy has rules, but you never do anything. I know Mommy won't let me put my juice here, but what about you? What are you going to do, put this coffee table out in the garage along with all your books?"

She gave me that cute little look of defiance in the form of a personal challenge. I'm embarrassed to say that my first response was to look out into the kitchen to see how much longer it was going to take Rosemary to get back out here and deal with *her* child.

Why are we so surprised when our children test the boundaries that we set before them? A healthy child will want to know if the boundary is for real. A healthy parenting plan will establish those boundaries rather than attempt to avoid confrontation at all costs.

Parenting with a Plan

To parent our children means that we are to prepare them for society. The world awaiting them is not devoid of boundaries and consequences. Our job as parents is to teach them about those boundaries. And that job is easier and more effective when we follow a disciplinary parenting plan that focuses on three basic concepts: responsibility, consistency, and love.

The responsibility for accepting the outcome of his behavior must be placed squarely on the child's shoulders. Boundaries must be established and consistently maintained. Finally, the child must know he is loved, regardless of his behavior.

It's important to base this plan on one of the commandments for life that God gave to the children of Israel: "Honor your father and mother." Respect is not an attitude that comes naturally to children. One mother, we'll call her Judy, came to me to discuss her four-year-old. "I don't know what happens to Tommy when I take him out in public.

The minute we get into a grocery store he becomes uncontrollable. It embarrasses me to death," she said.

Judy went on to say that her little boy would see something he wanted like cookies or candy. His first approach was to beg. When that did not work, he quickly moved on to other techniques such as throwing himself down on the grocery store floor and screaming.

I asked her whether Tommy did this at home. "Oh," she replied, "when he does that at home, I just leave the room until he stops. Sometimes it goes on for twenty minutes, and then I'm late with dinner. In the grocery store, however, I'm so embarrassed that I usually end up buying him the things he wants."

Obviously little Tommy had learned the system well. Mom had not established any boundaries, and that meant Tommy had not been taught to honor or respect his parent. Judy's number-one rule was to avoid conflict at all cost. At home that meant she left the room. At the store, she bought him his heart's desire.

Judy was actually teaching her child to rebel. The commandment, on the other hand, says just the opposite. Honor and respect are attitudes children must be taught.

Had Tommy learned to be self-centered from Judy's parenting? No, he was born self-centered. He had, however, learned how to feed his self-centered desires by manipulating Judy with his temper tantrums.

Before she could begin to help Tommy change the pattern of behavior he was displaying, she had to have a disciplinary plan based on responsibility, consistency, and love. The next three chapters will be devoted to those concepts.

Summary

1. A consistent plan of discipline must be established so that parent and child can love each other.

2. Discipline is necessary so each child can reach his or her full potential.

3. It is the job of the healthy, inquisitive child to rebel against the rules.

4. It is the job of the parent to handle this rebellion with a consistent plan.

3

Who Is Responsible?

IN MANY HOMES parents accept far too much responsibility for their child's behavior. Pete and Diane were parents that shouldered all the responsibility for the behavior and consequences of their son, Nathan. Nathan was supposed to do many things around the house, but he never quite got any of them done.

Nathan's behavioral patterns progressed to a point where he wasn't even getting up in the morning without a major confrontation. His parents came for help when it got to the point that Nathan was being sent to the office at his school for tardiness.

"I don't know how we have gotten to this point," Nathan's dad lamented. "He is basically a wonderful boy, but we end up arguing about everything. He can't even get out of bed in the morning without a fight."

Parents and child now argued over every issue. The basic question here was, "Who is responsible for Nathan's behavior?"

Pete and Diane were asked about the morning situation, since that seemed to be the most crucial to them at the moment. "Who holds the responsibility for Nathan to get out of bed in the morning, you or Nathan?" I asked.

"I know what you're thinking," Diane cried, "but we don't coddle Nathan. We try to give him as much responsibility as we can. It is supposed to be his responsibility to get up in the morning. I only go in and wake him up."

"You go into his room one time each morning to wake him up?" I asked.

"Well, not really," Diane replied. "I usually go in five or six times. By the fifth time, he's still in bed. I end up almost crazy, yelling and screaming at him."

11

"What do you do when Nathan doesn't get out of bed after you call him the first time?" I asked. In other words, "What is the consequence?"

"I've thrown cold water on him; in fact, I've tried everything," Diane answered. "We thought that if we let him go without waking him, the school would punish him for being late, but even that hasn't worked."

This illustration is typical of the frustration many parents and their children go through, and it also serves as an excellent example of misplaced responsibility.

At first, these parents stated that it was Nathan's responsibility to get up. Then they took it back and went in his room repeatedly, begging or screaming each morning. Actually, that was his only consequence. He was forced to start each day listening to his parents demean themselves as they begged him to get up. Then they demeaned and insulted him by yelling and screaming when he did not get up.

When Pete and Diane felt they could not get Nathan out of bed, they once again transferred the responsibility, but they did not give it back to Nathan. They decided to let the school deal with him for being late each morning. Nathan had not yet fallen under a plan that made him responsible for his behavior.

Yelling is not an appropriate or effective consequence. Worse than that, yelling teaches nothing positive to the child and destroys the parent-child relationship. If a state trooper pulled people over for speeding and only lectured them instead of issuing tickets, people would probably ignore the speed limits. Speeders would quickly learn to endure the lectures and listen to the officer with a glassy-eyed, inattentive attitude. Once the lecture was completed the citizen would drive off and forget about the incident. No real consequence would occur. The citizen would not be held accountable to accept a consequence, just a lecture.

Nathan was in the same situation. He was not held responsible for his behavior; his parents were. They were responsible for deciding how many times to go into Nathan's bedroom, how loud to yell, and whether or not to throw ice water. Basically, these parents had become Nathan's own personal snooze alarm. He just waited for the noise to get louder and louder.

A New Plan

Pete and Diane were sent home with something new. For the first time they had a real parenting plan. They called Nathan to the dining-room table to explain how it would work in their home. They began with an apology.

A: *State the Reason for the New Plan.*

"Nathan," Pete began, "I want to apologize to you for the way we have handled the mornings. We have been yelling at each other every morning for months. I'm sorry that we have operated this home in such a manner that everyone started the days in a bad mood."

These parents started the meeting by making Nathan aware of the fact that the old way of doing things was destructive to the family. Weeks later I talked to Nathan, and he told me that he was shocked at his parents' apologetic approach.

"When they called me to the table after they had been to see you, I was expecting another lecture," Nathan said. "You know, I just figured they were going to yell at me a little more. I was shocked when Dad said he was sorry. I was prepared for the yelling, but when he said he was sorry, I really started to listen. I knew that either something big was about to happen or that Dad had lost it!" (Nathan was making a reference to his father's mental stability.)

B: *Explain the Plan.*

Once Pete secured his son's attention, it was time to explain the plan. "Tomorrow morning we will institute a new morning plan. Your mother will come in *one* time, at seven o'clock, to wake you up. Neither of us will treat you like a baby by coming back into the bedroom. Breakfast will be on the table at 7:15, and we will expect you to be at the table with us. If you are not at the table for breakfast, then there will be no breakfast before school; that is *your* choice.

"If for some reason you choose not to get out of bed, one of us will come into your room after breakfast and help you get up. We will stand there until you are dressed and help you out the door without yelling. Do you have any questions?"

At this point, Nathan was scratching his head. It didn't sound too severe. Missing breakfast was no big deal; he had done that for months. After all, this was just one more new rule. Months ago Nathan's parents had tried to motivate him with something they heard about on the radio—a chart on the refrigerator and "smiley faces." And months before that his mother found a special formula of parent-child negotiations for behavior that they had tried to institute. This new plan didn't sound much different.

C: *The Consequence.*

"If you have no questions," Nathan's dad continued, "I need to tell you what will happen if you don't get up and come to the breakfast table by 7:15. If you cannot get up, we will assume that we have not been good parents. If you can't get up, it will say to me that you are not getting enough sleep at night and that 9:30 is too late a bedtime for you right now.

"On the mornings that you don't come to the breakfast table by 7:15, you will go to bed at 7:30 that night."

D: *Placing Total Responsibility on the Child's Shoulders.*

"Nathan, I want to make sure you understand what will happen when you don't get up on time."

"You will make me go to bed early," Nathan responded.

"No," his father said emphatically. "*You* will be making yourself go to bed early. If you can't get up in the morning, it will be as if you say to us, 'Mom and Dad, 9:30 is too late for me to stay up; I need more sleep.' You will now be the one who is responsible for your bedtime. I will only enforce the plan. If you can't get up, you will go to bed early, but that will be your responsibility. Do you understand?"

Nathan said nothing, so his father continued.

"You will also be responsible for one other part of your bedtime. When you do make it to breakfast for a week straight, and I really hope you do so that we can be together, then your behavior will say to us, 'I can handle my 9:30 bedtime; how about extending it to 10:00?' Once again, that will be your choice. You will be responsible for that decision."

Obviously the key concept to begin to teach the child is that the choices are in his hands. Yes, the parent will enforce the consequences, but the child will be in a position to make the decisions. The child will be held accountable and will be responsible for his decisions.

Teaching the proper understanding of discipline necessitates placing responsibility for decisions and consequences on the child's shoulders. When it is done in the appropriate manner, the child will learn to discipline himself. This is the goal of the parents' plan.

Summary

1. The parent must establish a plan for dealing with behavior and then explain it to the child.

2. The parent must explain the consequence for unacceptable behavior.

3. The parent must place the responsibility for the child's behavior directly on the child's shoulders.

4. The parent must be consistent in handling this plan.

4

"We Argue about Everything!"

"WHEN I TELL HIM to do something or ask him not to do something, everything is OK. He seems to understand. It appears that way until he actually goes ahead and breaks the rule. At that point we always seem to argue. What must I do to stop this arguing?"

This plea was from a parent who established a plan for her child, but when it got right down to it, she decided not to live by it. She would say to her child, who had broken a prearranged family rule, "Oh, OK. We won't make you go to bed this time, but next time you'll go to bed early for sure. And I mean it this time."

The child in a home like this quickly realizes that the rules don't count. He doesn't have to obey. His main objective is to figure out how to deal with, coerce, beg, or manipulate Mom. No matter what Mom or Dad may say is the plan, he knows better. This child has no personal responsibility. His parents maintain the responsibility since they decide whether or not they want to reinforce the rules.

Operating in this manner abuses the child as well as the family. It actually encourages a child to argue with his parents.

Suppose a state trooper pulled you over for speeding. You knew that you had been speeding and deserved the ticket. But when the trooper approached your car, you recognized him as the one who could be encouraged to withhold the ticket if you argued with him. I hope that everyone reading this book would respond to this situation by being responsible enough to accept the consequence without arguing. I seriously doubt that this would be the case, however. The mere fact that you know he may withhold the consequence if you argue with him is tempting.

The same is true with the child. The temptation is far too great for him, also. If he knows that his parent is inconsistent about handling the rules, then he is actually encouraged to argue. He benefits more from arguing than from remaining quiet and accepting the consequences for his behavior. Setting him up to argue is like setting him up to destroy his relationship with his parents. It's simply not fair.

Consistency Is the Key

Consistency is the key to getting out from under the arguments. The state trooper has too many "children" to watch to be able to consistently enforce the rules. Because of this dilemma, many people consciously speed. They know that he is not always there. Let's say, for the sake of making a point, that the government decided to install an ominous little black box in the dashboards of all automobiles in the United States. This box had only one purpose: to measure the speed of the car, give off a beep every time the driver exceeded the speed limit, and for each occurrence punch out a ticket that must be paid within ten days. After a driver received one or two quick tickets, it would be amazing how careful he would become at obeying the speed limit.

Why would he drive in a more responsible manner? Simply because his behavior was now being handled in a more consistent way. Consistent handling of the plan is the way to place the responsibility for the outcome on the right shoulders.

Pete and Diane did a good job of explaining the new plan to Nathan. But as Nathan said, they had done a good job of explaining plans in the past. The placement of responsibility had not taken place yet.

Pete and Diane were both excited about the way their family meeting had gone. Nathan seemed to understand all that was said. Surely, they thought, he will understand and pop out of bed in the morning.

The next morning came and Diane went into the kitchen to start breakfast. Since this was going to be such a special breakfast, she went all out, preparing sausage and scrambled eggs. Then she went into Nathan's room and sat on the side of his bed for a moment while she woke him up. "Are you up, Nathan?" she asked before leaving his room. He assured her that he was and that he would be at the table for breakfast. So Diane returned to the kitchen to continue making this special meal.

An interesting thing took place while Diane was in the kitchen. She noticed that Nathan wasn't making a peep. Perhaps he wasn't getting up, she thought. At that moment Pete came into the kitchen, himself responding to the new plan to be at the breakfast table by 7:15. He immediately noticed his wife's consternation.

"What's wrong, Honey?" Pete asked.

"I woke Nathan up at seven," Diane responded, sounding discouraged, "but I don't hear any noises coming from his room. Maybe he didn't hear me. Maybe he didn't really understand what we told him last night. I think one of us should go back in and make sure he's getting up."

"Snooze alarm," Pete said.

"What?" Diane asked. "What in the world are you talking about?"

"Do you remember what the counselor said we are doing when we keep going back into his room to get him up? He said we were taking the responsibility back from Nathan. That basically we were becoming his own personal snooze alarm and that he really did not need to learn to get up for himself as long as we were willing to do it for him. Diane, we've got to let him learn the hard way. That means sticking to the original plan that we have already explained to him."

Diane was discouraged. She had been sure the plan would work. Seeing this, Pete tried to comfort her with the joke they had been told about the probable sequence of events for that morning. "Do you remember that the counselor jokingly told us there was a special posture you were supposed to go into while you were cooking the breakfast? He said that after you had gone in to wake Nathan, you were to immediately extend your arm out perpendicular from your body as if to signal a left-hand turn and keep it there, or the new plan would not work. Remember how we both looked at him like he was crazy and how he went on to say that you must cook the eggs and set the table with this one arm extended and not let it down until you sit down to eat? We laughed when he said that the extended arm would make it impossible for you to go back into Nathan's room to wake him up again. Your body would not fit through the doorway to his room.

"We laughed then, but now we can see his point. It was really just a warning. He knew that the plan would not work until it had been tested. Nathan is testing the plan."

Diane was discouraged that the first morning of the new plan was just like all the rest: no Nathan. She was also sorry that his eggs went to waste.

After breakfast Pete and Diane went into Nathan's bedroom together and woke him up. He slowly got out of bed and noticed that something was different. His parents were in his room, but there was no yelling and screaming. They stood over him while he got dressed, and they sent him out the door to school. Nathan was shocked to find out what time it was and that it was too late for breakfast. He had expected them to come into his room several times before breakfast. But now all they said was, "Sorry, Honey, you missed breakfast." He couldn't get over how pleasant they were.

Nathan went off to school startled, and Diane remained home discouraged. Once again she felt like a failure. But the plan had not really gone into effect yet.

After school an interesting thing took place. Nathan was more pleasant than usual. As the dinner hour rolled around he even volunteered to help set the table. This was absolutely unheard of. Maybe he had hit his head during the day, his mom thought. When dinner was over, he actually took his plate from the table to the kitchen counter without being asked. Then Nathan helped, ever so slightly, with the dishes.

Then came the crowning blow. Nathan asked his mom if she would like to play checkers with him after the dishes were done. It had been years since Nathan had asked her to do anything but iron his favorite shirt. But Diane was prepared for this moment and had rehearsed to herself what to say.

"Nathan, I would love to play checkers with you more than do anything else tonight; but unfortunately you have chosen to go to bed early. That means it's almost time for you to go take your shower."

If there is a crucial time for the placement of responsibility, it is at this point in the plan. I remember seeing a movie years ago where two soldiers, on opposing sides, were in their foxholes throwing the same grenade back and forth to each other. One had pulled the pin and thrown it at the other. The other man picked it up and quickly threw it back to where it came from. This went on, back and forth, for quite some time. For obvious reasons neither soldier wanted to be left holding the grenade.

This is similar to the volley that went on between Nathan and his mother. No sooner did Diane tell Nathan that he had chosen to go to bed early that night than the volley began. Neither person wanted to be left holding the responsibility for Nathan's not getting out of bed at the proper time that morning.

Nathan began with, "Oh, Mom, please, I forgot. I forgot about what you said last night. Please, just give me one more chance. I promise. Tomorrow morning if I don't get up I'll go to bed after school." Nathan did everything he could to pass the responsibility for his behavior on to his mother. He begged and pleaded, but Diane would not allow him to dump the responsibility on her.

"Nathan, when you made the decision not to get out of bed and come to breakfast, you made the decision to go to bed at this early hour. It's not fair for you to try to make me feel bad. I'm not the one to talk to about this."

"But Mom, it's still light outside. No one could possibly go to sleep at this hour." Nathan's response had moved from pleading to complaining.

"Don't talk to me about it, Nathan. You made the decision."

Nathan's parents saw to it that he got to bed that night by 7:30. They spoke no harsh words. They simply did two things. First they went into his room after he went to bed and sat on the side of his bed. Nathan, of course, initially took this as a sign that they had changed their mind. When he saw his mom come in, he thought she was going to tell him he could get up. That was not the case, however. The second thing Diane did was to talk to Nathan and encourage him.

"Nathan, there is nothing I would like to do more than play checkers with you. Please do your best to get up at the proper time tomorrow so we can be together. But remember this, Honey, if you once again choose not to get up and get to breakfast by 7:15 tomorrow, you will be telling us that you still need more sleep. Please don't make us put you to bed at 7:30 again tomorrow. I'm not going to argue with you anymore in the mornings though. I love you too much to treat you like that. It will be your responsibility to get up after I call you."

Nathan went to sleep that night. He wasn't happy about the early bedtime. The next morning Diane was convinced that Nathan would have learned his lesson. Not so! He had to be convinced that they weren't going to give in and drop the plan.

Three weeks later, just as Diane had reached a point of feeling defeated, the first sign of light was seen. For three weeks Nathan had not shown any signs of changing. For three weeks Pete and Diane had followed the plan. For three weeks Nathan had gone to bed at 7:30, and every night he had tried to pass the responsibility on to them. "I'll bet I'm the only kid in America whose parents make him go to bed so early."

Pete responded, in a kind but firm voice, "Correction. I'll bet you're the only kid in America who makes his parents put him to bed at 7:30."

That next morning, at 7:14-and-a-half Nathan showed up at the breakfast table. It was not the way his parents would have liked him to arrive. His hair stuck out on one side, his breath was horrible, and his clothes were only half on, but he was there. He had finally made the attempt.

On the other end, however, breakfast was not quite what Nathan wanted. Two weeks ago the eggs and sausages had been abandoned for cold cereal. No use wasting the eggs.

Nathan's parents did the right thing, though. Disheveled or not, they went wild, thanking him for making it to breakfast and letting him know how much it meant to the whole family when they could all start their day together.

Nathan finished dressing, and as he went out the door his mother called him back, gave him a kiss, and said, "Thank you for making my day."

It had been a long time since Nathan had made anyone's day, so in order to hear it again he responded with, "How'd I do that, Mom?"

It was as if for three weeks Nathan had lined himself up in front of a brick wall, put his head down, and run toward it at full speed. In years past his parents had told him that he would hit his head; but then they ran out in front of him and moved the wall. For three weeks the wall had not been moved by his parents. What they said, they meant. It finally occurred to him that he was doing it to himself. It was as if he said to himself, "Why do I keep hitting my head on this wall?"

Nathan finally realized that his parents loved him enough to stick with the plan. If he didn't want to go to bed early, it was up to him to get up on time. And besides, it was nice to see how happy it made his parents.

Consistency is everything when establishing boundaries for children. Otherwise there aren't really any boundaries, only rules that depend on the whims of the parents rather than the behavior of the children. That kind of plan, or lack of a plan, causes arguments; it abuses rather than instructs.

Ephesians 6:4 talks about setting up a plan that will not exasperate and discourage children when it says: "And now a word to you parents. Don't keep on scolding and nagging your children, making them angry and resentful" (TLB).

Constant nagging doesn't change their behavior. In contrast, a plan that places the responsibility on the child's shoulders will not only change his behavior, it will also help prepare him for the adult world. His boss will not call him at home in the morning and gently say, "Excuse me, Nathan, is that you? I don't mean to wake you, but it's 10:00 A.M. and you're two hours late for work again. Do you think you could come in to work this morning?"

That will very likely not be the boss's approach. If Nathan is not able to accept the responsibility, he will unfortunately need to accept the consequences of hearing the words, "You are fired!" The purpose of childhood is to help him learn to be able to accept responsibility.

Summary

1. The parent must be secure enough in the fact that the plan is fair and stick with it.

2. The parent must make sure the plan is instructional. In other words, the child should eventually learn something from the plan that will help him cope with life.

3. The plan must place the burden of responsibility on the child's shoulders no matter how hard he works to throw it back.

4. The parent must stick to the plan in a consistent and objective manner.

5. Nagging and ridiculing are not part of the plan.

6. If you constantly argue, chances are you have not been consistent.

5

Don't Become Part of the Consequence

CHILDHOOD DEPRESSION is on the rise, according to the National Institute of Mental Health. More than ever before children are finding it difficult to deal with this world that surrounds them. In past generations children were allowed to remain children for longer periods of time, and were, for the most part, shielded from the world of adults.

The world of the child is drastically different today. Our society forces children to know about the difficulties and travesties of the adult world through the medium of television. Long before they are emotionally prepared to deal with the adult world, the child is thrust into it.

Childhood depression may stem from this relative loss of innocence. I have often heard children express other reasons for these feelings of melancholy. The most disturbing, however, is the child who has come to feel that no one is on his side. Many children have actually come to believe their parents are against them or even their adversaries.

"My parents yell at me all the time. It's easier to go down the street and hang out at Mr. Black's house until it's time for me to go home. I usually stay just as long as I can."

The saddest thing that happens in so many homes today is that some children feel like they must go to the home of a stranger in order to hear a kind word said to them. Little wonder that it is estimated that 6 to 7 percent of today's youth suffer from clinical depression.

Handle Behavior Objectively

Parents must learn to separate the handling of the child's behavior from their response to the child himself. When the people who brought the child into this world are the ones who berate, ridicule, and yell

23

at him, three things take place. First, the child is made to feel personally worthless. Second, the lines of communication between parent and child are broken. And third, the parents who do the berating render themselves ineffective. By berating, ridiculing, or yelling at the child, the parent actually becomes the consequence for the child's unacceptable behavior.

Behavior must be handled in an objective manner. The child, on the other hand, must know that he is loved at all times. He must feel as if his parents are on his side, pulling for his success. Anything less than that is emotional child abuse.

Think of a professional football game. The players on the field are the best in the world. They know the rules better than any spectator. They know they can't go out of bounds or the play is over. Despite all they know, however, we still put seven officials (parents, if you will) out there on that field, with striped shirts on, to enforce the rules.

The key to objective intervention can be seen by watching the way a referee handles an infraction of the rules. He does not raise his voice and scream at the player, saying, "You idiot! That was the worst attempt at football I've ever seen. Aren't you ever going to play this game correctly? I don't even know why I bother with you."

That approach would not be very effective. Instead, he stops the action, confronts the player by announcing the violation, and calmly issues the consequence for the violation. The player knew ahead of time what that consequence would be.

At this point it is once again left up to the player as to whether he wants to argue or not. He may question the ruling and ask for an explanation, but if he crosses the line of propriety, he will once again, in a calm manner, be penalized.

The referee deals with the behavior of the player rather than with the player. It is the same way the state trooper is taught to deal with speeders on the highway. He is taught to calmly pull the driver over, ask to see his license, announce the infraction, and issue the ticket. The officer is not to say, "In all my years that's the worst driving I have ever seen. How old are you, anyway? You drive like you have the brains of a three-year-old."

The state trooper issues the consequence, politely returns the driver's license, and may even say, "Please have a safe trip." You are not led to believe that he is against you. In fact, you may drive away feeling as if he actually cares about your well-being.

This kind of attitude is even more significant for parents to adopt as part of their plan for handling discipline. Nathan's parents did not get the desired result to their plan the first morning. When he did not get out of bed, his mother was tempted, out of habit, to go into his bedroom again and start yelling. That was her natural response and her mode of operation from the past.

When parents find themselves yelling at their child, it is a sign of many things. It says that they probably don't actually have a plan. It is a sign that they are frustrated and are meeting their own need to let off steam. It is a sign that they really don't yet have a sincere desire to help their child change his behavior. Yelling and screaming may make a parent think he has handled the situation for the moment, but it really just postpones any long-term opportunity for change. The child fears the parent but does not understand any principles that will help him learn to accept responsibility.

Pete and Diane established a plan for Nathan's behavior. If he did not get up at the appropriate time, the consequence was early bedtime that night. Nowhere in that plan did it say that Diane was to berate her son if he did not get up on time. Nowhere in the plan did it say that Diane should send her son off to school with, "You just wait until tonight. I hope you haven't forgotten that you are going to pay for this infraction. You are just so stupid."

In fact, the plan allows Diane to give her son a kiss as he goes off to school. It is imperative that the child feels like his parents are on his side. The fact that parents have a plan they feel confident in allows them to loosen up and love the child.

It is mandatory that parents make a determined effort to decide which side of the fence they will be on in handling discipline. It is too devastating when they become part of the consequence by causing their children to feel as if Mom and Dad are withdrawing love as part of the punishment. A consequence handled in an objective manner leaves the parent free to be on the child's side, pulling for him to do better.

The first night that Nathan was sent to bed early, Diane added one more idea to her disciplinary plan. Though her child was sent to bed early, she did not need to isolate herself from him. Instead, she went into his room, after he had been sent to bed, and sat on the side of his bed. Most children would immediately think that the parent was reversing the decision, taking back the responsibility for their behavior, and about to allow them to get out of bed.

At this point a parent can reassure the child that "I wish I could let you out of bed. I gain no pleasure by watching you go to bed early. But this was your decision, not mine. Please don't choose to do this again so that we can all be together tomorrow night. Now roll over and let me rub your back."

A father once told me that he felt this approach was like showing a sign of weakness. Obviously he had set himself up as his child's adversary. "A sign of weakness to whom, the enemy?" I asked him. Your child is not on the opposing side. That is what you must teach him. If a parent has a plan he feels comfortable with and handles it consistently, he can place himself on the child's side.

Spending time sitting on the side of the child's bed would not be a sign of weakness. It would be a sign of love. The purpose is to deal with the behavior while loving the child.

Love Him, No Matter What . . .

It is significant that the child comes to a point where he realizes that no matter what he does, he will be held responsible for his behavior. But it is even more significant that a child sees that his parents love him, no matter what he does.

Remember John Hinckley, Jr.? He came from a fine Christian home where he was taught right from wrong by his parents. In the early part of President Reagan's first term, this young man shocked the nation when he shot the president.

It is safe to say that this young man had never done anything that could have disappointed and embarrassed his parents more than this one event. I'm sure that they spent weeks, and maybe more, in tears. They were hounded by reporters and went through a horrible form of societal punishment because of their son's behavior.

Listening to them talk on television gave me a special appreciation for this hurting couple. I gained even more appreciation for them as I watched the trial of their son. No matter what his behavior, no matter what pain he caused in their lives, he was obviously still their son. He was on trial to face the consequence of his actions, and there they were, sitting with him for all the world to see. They certainly did not support his behavior, but they were there to support their son.

This is a beautiful picture of how a parent must deal with a child's unacceptable behavior: Attack the behavior, not the child. This is not a new concept; it's been around since the beginning of time. Our heavenly Father established a behavioral plan for His children to live by. This plan was for mankind's own good and development.

God gave these behavioral boundaries to Moses in the form we know as the Ten Commandments. As mankind violated these behavioral rules, the consequences had to be faced. One consequence was too steep for man to have to face, however. When an individual sins or chooses to go against the preestablished rules for behavior, the ultimate consequence is to be cut off from God.

Since our heavenly Father, in His perfection as the Creator, cannot look upon sin, when a person sins he is in essence choosing to pull away from the Father's love. The Father, in response, attacked the problem while loving His children. He sent His only Son, Jesus Christ, to pay the consequence for our sin. Mankind did not deserve such love. Yet the Father chose to love us while dealing with our rebellious behavior.

This is a perfect example from a perfect Father. Our job is to emulate that formula: Deal with the behavior while loving the child. That way it will eventually become obvious to the child that his parents are on his side.

Summary

1. Be objective about the disciplinary plan.

2. Decide ahead of time how you will react to your child if he tests your sincerity and violates the plan.

3. Decide not to allow yourself to become a part of the consequence that your child must face. Don't yell and scream.

4. Once the consequence has been handled, you are free to jump on his side. Take time to love him.

6

Ethnic Traits That Help

I HAD THE PRIVILEGE of growing up on Long Island in an area where most of my friends were of Italian descent. Spending time in their homes was always a feast of culture, pasta, and emotions. In the home of one close friend with whom I actually spent a summer, there were three generations living under the same roof.

This Italian family was very exciting to be around. Everything was a major event to them. When you showed up for dinner, the grand-mother acted as if she hadn't seen you in ages, even though you had eaten breakfast with her family that day. She would hug everybody and talk loudly about how good it was for all of us to be together. She treated every event as if it was a major happening. She made every person around her feel special.

This kind of expressiveness was always quite a change for me. Growing up in a German home meant that we were much more reserved in our handling of emotions. The classic German might not have seen a family member since the previous summer vacation, and yet they would greet each other with an objective handshake. You would rarely see any emotion. When Uncle Mike came home, after spending a year away from us, one would think he had just returned from a trip to the bathroom.

If a typical German clan had ever eaten a meal with my friend's family and all their expressiveness, the Germans would have had an instant attack of high blood pressure. The difference in the way my family and this Italian family expressed themselves always amazed me.

Crazy with Emotion

One night, while I was staying with my friend, there was a major disruption. At least I interpreted it as a major disruption. Connie, his sixteen-year-old sister, was due home from a night out with friends. She was supposed to be home at ten, and it was eleven-thirty, with no sign of her.

Everyone in the house was absolutely crazy with emotion. The older adults reverted to their native tongue as they shouted to each other about what might have happened to Connie. They bounced back and forth from the catastrophe that Connie might have been involved in to what they were going to do to her when she finally did come home. They were so wild that I was convinced that there was no disaster out in the streets that could have been worse than what Connie was going to face when she finally did return.

At ten to twelve Connie walked in the door. In a matter of seconds the adults in charge surmised that she was all right. Once that was established, they went absolutely crazy. The yelling and screaming were unbelievable. Without a doubt every neighbor for blocks knew what Connie had done, and for about half an hour we all heard the list of consequences she faced.

I went up to bed that night with my friend feeling sorry for all the punishments this girl was going to have to endure. As we were lying in bed, I said to my friend, "What do you think Connie will do?"

"About what?" he asked.

"About not being able to go out of the house for the rest of the summer," I replied.

"Oh, they'll forget about that by breakfast. You watch. When we get up tomorrow, everybody will act like nothing ever happened."

"You've got to be kidding," I answered. "I thought they were going to kill her down there in the living room."

"Yeah, that's the way my folks always act when they're mad at us. They yell and scream and threaten all these terrible things that are going to happen. Then a few hours later it's back to normal and no punishment," he said.

Not this time, I thought to myself as we went off to sleep. I was there; I heard the threats. In fact, the whole town probably heard the threats. There was no way they could simply be forgotten by morning.

I almost regretted having to be present the next morning for the continued confrontation that I anticipated would take place at breakfast. I walked downstairs and into the kitchen, and the family was back to its jolly self. Then in walked Connie, and I could not believe the scene. Everyone kissed as they always did and breakfast proceeded as usual.

My friend grinned across the table at the amazement on my face. He was right. Connie's behavior had generated lots of talk and emotion, but no real consequence. It was so different from my German background.

I remember wondering which I would like better: a family that hugged all the time and made a major deal out of everything, or a family that never got excited about anything but never yelled at you, either.

Blending Both Extremes

Actually a blend would be perfect. What if a family responded in both ethnic extremes? Parents could get excited about everything the children did. They could be Italian about a child's projects and announce to the neighborhood how proud they were of little Johnny. Instead of shaking hands they could constantly hug and touch each other.

These Italian expressions of love make children feel special. The constant hugging and touching lets them know they are a special part of the family.

Far too often families live in one mode or the other. The child either gets lots of expressiveness from his family or he gets no attention at all. He gets built up and then ripped apart, or he gets ignored.

In other families, both ethnic principles are used—but the parents have them reversed. When little Johnny is on task, doing what he is supposed to be doing, they hardly acknowledge his existence. They adopt the German approach and say very little. In other words, when Johnny is good, he is often handled in an objective manner.

When he is bad, however, the Italian comes out, and the child is berated and screamed at. Some children never see any emotion directed toward them until they have broken a rule. Then the emotion they receive from their parents is all negative.

Working at Sheridan House Family Ministries, I have seen many children come into our care who have adopted the philosophy that negative attention is better than no attention at all. These children had learned that they were never going to get any word at all from Mom or Dad unless they did something to get screamed at. As warped as that kind of attention is, it was all some of these children had experienced, and they considered it better than nothing.

That's backward. It's just the opposite of the way we should treat our children. We should shower them with love and attention all the time. We should all be like my friend's Italian grandmother in the way we express our love for our children, except when our children need to be reprimanded. At that point we need to cross the Alps and become German, handling the discipline in an objective manner. In other words, as parents we need to be Italian about the love and affection we show our children, and German in the way we handle discipline.

The coach in my old high school was an expert with this concept. For one reason or another when I was a student, I was constantly being sent down to his office for a paddling. He never gave me lengthy lectures or berated me in any way. He was very objective in the way he handled the consequences. When it was done, he never mentioned it again. In fact, he went overboard to build me up.

At the end of the school day, Coach always stood outside the front of the school as all of us got on the bus. On those days when I'd been sent to his office, he would walk over to me, and in front of all my friends, Coach would find something nice to say about me while he had a hand on my shoulder. I always felt ten feet tall when he did that. Somehow I forgot that this was the man who had just paddled me. He was German about the discipline but Italian about our relationship.

"How do you do that?" one parent asked me. "Sometimes he makes me so mad that I don't feel like loving him."

That parent was incapable of being objective about the discipline of the child because she took his disruptive behavior as a personal affront. This mom took it personally when her child did not do as he was told. It was not that he was breaking *the rules,* it was that he was breaking *her* rules, on purpose, just to make her mad. Or so she thought.

Many parents are like that with their children. They are accustomed to the business world where they tell an employee to do or not to do something and are shocked if they have to tell him again. Bring that mentality home and you take it as a personal attack when Junior misbehaves: "I can't believe he just did that. I've already told him that was not allowed."

Handling Discipline Objectively

Most of the time Junior doesn't do those things to attack his parents. It's not a personal affront. He's simply testing the boundaries. We can't expect children to respond like employees. Employees are adults; children are children. Our Lord loaned them to us to raise for eighteen years, not just for one simple lecture on rules and regulations.

Once a parent understands that Junior is not making a personal attack, then a parent can begin to handle the consequences in a more objective manner. He can get the consequences out of the way and get back to loving the child.

"But it is at just those times that I don't feel like loving my child," you might say.

I am quite sure that my coach didn't feel like expressing love to me many of those afternoons, but he went out of his way to do it anyway. Not because he felt like it, but because he knew I needed it.

I think it was Karen Mains who I heard say once, "When love is the hardest for a parent to give, love is probably the most needed by the child." What a true statement. Children need love most when they feel they have done something to damage the relationship they have or want to have with their parents. A child especially needs to be loved when he feels unlovable. When he has done something wrong, when his attitude is the least lovely, that is the time he needs an outward expression of love.

When disciplinary action is necessary, the child is not only anxious about the consequence but also about the loss of love. A parent needs to handle the situation in such a way that the child realizes there is no love withdrawn. Handling discipline with an objective attitude and then moving on to a subjective atmosphere helps the child know he is special and valuable.

What comes after the consequences is important: the reestablishing of the relationship, the reassuring of the child that he is forgiven and loved, and the building of the child's confidence in his value to the family.

When my son was four, we had a problem keeping him in bed at night. It had come to the point where we had to establish a consequence with him. He knew that if he got out of bed in the middle of the night to play, he would be warned once, then spanked.

One night Rosemary and I were getting ready to leave to go out to dinner. The baby-sitter had arrived and Robey was in bed asleep, or so I thought. I opened the door to his room to check on him before we left. Robey has always been a very heavy sleeper, so I could turn on his light and it would not wake him. I had gotten into a habit of doing that so I could just look at my youngest child for a moment while he lay sleeping.

This particular night I turned on the light, and the bed was empty. Then I heard an airplane noise coming from his big closet. I opened the door to the closet only to find my son dressed in his Superman pajamas, cape and all, climbing up the shelves to reach some of his airplanes. I startled him and caught this little Superman as he started to fall from about four feet up the shelves.

His eyes were big as golf balls as I put him back in bed. And I remember saying, "Robey, what will Daddy have to do if you get out of bed again tonight?"

"I'll have to get a 'pank, Daddy," was his reply.

"That's right, Honey. Please don't make me do that. Please stay in bed."

I gave Robey a kiss, tucked him in, and left his room. I wanted to turn this matter over to the baby-sitter, but I knew whose responsibility it was. I knew that I needed to go back down the hall.

Now there are two ways I could have gone back down the hall: I could have (and would liked to have) clumped down the hall so loudly that my son would have hopped back in bed. Under those conditions when I would have asked him if he was out of bed, Robey would have been tempted to say, "Oh, no, Daddy."

To avoid putting my child in that position, I chose the alternative. I quietly walked down the hall to his room, hoping that he was sound asleep. As I opened the bedroom door, I saw a three-foot Superman flying across the room from the closet to the bed. He lay there with his eyes squeezed closed, pretending to be asleep.

I wanted to pretend, too—that I thought he was asleep. But I knew that wasn't part of the deal. I walked over to his bed and said calmly, "Robey, I'll be right back."

He knew that meant I was going into the kitchen to get the wooden spoon. When I came back into the room, I spanked him once with the spoon, put the spoon down, and said, "Honey, why did Daddy have to do that?"

"Because I got out of bed," he said as he cried.

"That's right, Robey. I hate to do that, but I love you and if you disobey, you are forcing me to do just what I did. Please don't disobey anymore."

That was the German part of disciplining. Some child care experts tell us we should leave them alone for a while after they have been punished so that the event will sink in. I happen to believe that the events that follow the consequence are every bit as important as the consequence itself. For me, the next step was to get into the Italian mode of parenting.

Though we were about to be late for our dinner reservations, I knew that I could not just get up and walk out of Robey's room at that point. It was time to love him. I got down on his bed with him and held my son for a while. Soon he realized that I was not mad at him, and he was ready to sleep.

I'm not the consequence, so I don't have to withdraw from my child. In fact, quite the contrary is true. I need to be the Italian hugger in my home, most especially after we have had to deal with a negative event. Robey learned quickly not to get out of bed. That lesson is not so important, but he was able to learn another lesson at the same time. My son was able to see that I love him regardless of what he does. That lesson is very important. It will help us immensely as we deal with the more difficult disciplinary lessons during his eighteen or so years.

That concept of being loved unconditionally doesn't just happen for a child. It must be expressed over and over again. I encourage parents to adopt the best traits of two different ethnic groups when they respond to their children, being careful not to get their applications backward. They should be German about discipline and Italian about everything else.

Summary

1. Deal with your child's unacceptable behavior objectively and unemotionally, like a German.

2. Hand out love to your child, talk to your child, and hug your child constantly, like an Italian.

3. Children must see the difference in the way parents respond to good versus bad behavior.

4. Don't get the ethnic qualities backward. It's too damaging to get emotional about the discipline while ignoring good behavior.

5. Adopt these steps when your child is young, and it will help make discipline much easier when the child is older and the issues are more significant.

PART II

Parenthood: Getting Organized

7

Who Needs the Discipline?

"WOW! HOW DOES a parent remember all these things? I can't believe how organized I have to be to effectively parent my child." Some parents may be overwhelmed by the job of developing and implementing a disciplinary plan.

Anything that is worth doing takes thought. As I am writing this book, I am learning to use a computer. Prior to this my other books were done by applying pencil to paper. It was tedious, but that's the way I had always done my writing. Then someone bought me a computer. Using it has required a lot of thought and long hours to learn how it works; but now that time and work have paid off. This new knowledge and its application will have a tremendous impact on my future endeavors.

The same can be said about parenting with a plan. Taking the time to establish that plan will have a great impact in many areas of life, beginning with a better parent/child relationship.

A parent called me not long ago to tell me something very exciting. This lady and her husband had been sitting in their family room one night listening to some of our parenting tapes. While they were listening to the tapes, other ears were listening from the bedroom. The eleven-year-old daughter in this family was listening to her parents study and discuss the tapes.

It surprised her that her mom and dad took parenting so seriously. The next morning she told her mother, "I didn't realize you and Dad were trying so hard to be parents. I thought everything just kind of happened. I never really thought that you had a plan for us."

This child and her brother were fortunate in that their parents were working to design a plan for their training and thus for their future. The mother went on to tell me that her daughter had a suggestion. "Why don't you let us listen to the tapes with you?" the daughter asked.

"That way we will be able to understand what you are doing." She had a good point.

Staff Meetings

Everyone who is involved should understand what the plan is all about. We know that is necessary in every other area of life. Businesses have weekly staff meetings to make sure that they are still on target. Likewise, churches set aside time for staff meetings and calendar meetings to see to it that they are working in one direction.

If it is significant for businesses, churches, and even civic clubs to hold planning meetings, how much more significant must it be for families to conduct planning meetings. The success of the family—and the families of the next generation—might depend on it.

Effective discipline does not just happen. It is a planned program that must be established and maintained by the parent or parents. It requires prearranged staff meetings. Every New Year's Eve my wife, Rosemary, and I spend a couple of hours poring over a very significant file. It's called the Goals File. In it there are three pages, each covering a different area of our life, with goals we set for the year that is ending. One page has a list of spiritual goals, one lists financial goals, and the third lists marital and parenting goals.

Twelve months prior we had gotten together and established these goals for our lives and our children's growth. Throughout the year the two of us had gotten together for "staff" meetings to evaluate how we were doing. New Year's Eve was the deadline. That night we looked at our goals to see how we had done. Once we have finished with the previous year's goals, we bring in the New Year by getting the next year's goals on paper.

When and Where to Meet

Regular weekly "staff" meetings are the key to see to it that these goals are still being pursued. The meeting for us consists of a date either at home or at a restaurant for a cup of coffee. I have found that I do much better at concentrating on the meeting if I am out of the house. For some reason, when I am at home I become distracted much more easily. The phone interrupts, the television looks too inviting, or any of a variety of other activities distracts me there. Perhaps the worst is that special chair that seems to anesthetize me when my body makes contact with it. Once I'm sitting there, it's almost hopeless for anyone to try to communicate with me. Going out for a cup of coffee is not always feasible; but in our home, it is the best way for Rosemary and me to have a staff meeting.

What to Discuss

The logistics of the meeting itself are very significant. This is not a time for husband and wife to make accusations about incompetence. This is a time to discuss goals and how the team is going to reach those goals.

Perhaps a wife is concerned about their twelve-year-old daughter. Mom is noticing that the young girl is becoming more and more distant. The question that this parenting team should ask might be, "Are we reaching out to her at this time?" Perhaps each parent should decide to make an effort to be with this daughter in the coming weeks. Dad could decide to take her out to breakfast once a week, and Mom might invite her to share a walk around the block.

One mandatory piece of equipment at a parenting staff meeting is the family calendar. When decisions are made about *what* needs to be done, the next logical step is to decide *when* they will be done. A breakfast date with the twelve-year-old can then be put on the calendar.

When family problems of a more behavioral nature are discussed at staff meetings, a list of questions should be asked concerning the behavior.

1. *Is this behavior simply something that is just childish, though annoying, or is it an area that should be dealt with?* Billy is four years old and spills his milk every other meal. This is not a defiant behavior but more of a childish behavior that can probably be remedied by putting Billy's milk in a less tipsy cup or putting his cup in a better location on the table.

2. *Is this area of our child's personal discipline something that we need to deal with because it will have a lasting effect on his or her life?* Not cleaning his room, not being home when he's told to be, disobeying rules, and many other challenges to authority are areas that will have a lasting effect on the child's development. Length of hair may not be as significant.

3. *Are we trying to establish a rule that we are unable to enforce?* A frightening worry for parents is the choice of friends that their

teen-agers make. It is a fact that the peers our children spend their time with will have an impact on their attitudes and behaviors. With that in mind, many parents spend a great deal of time and energy attempting to tell their children those whom they *may not* hang around with. "And if I catch you with that person again, this is what the consequence will be," they say.

Children have so much freedom today that it is very unlikely that a parent will be able to enforce such a statement. Most likely, an attempt to do so will simply alienate the child and make his new friendship a martyr-type situation—their friendship against the world.

When a parent attempts to structure an area that he or she has little or no real control over, it only becomes frustrating for all concerned. The parent becomes frustrated because he feels out of control. The child becomes frustrated because he feels that the only way out of the situation is to lie about whether he is continuing to see this friend.

Is this area of concern something that parents can have an impact on, or do they need to offer advice and pray for God's protection?

4. *Is the behavior in question the child's way of signaling a need?* Perhaps the child's recent disciplinary problems in school are really only an outward manifestation of something else. Children generally find it difficult to say, "Excuse me, Mom, could we sit down and talk? I'm beginning to have peer problems, and I need to talk to you about how to handle my friends."

There are many possible reasons for disruptive behavior. A child may not know how to express what he's dealing with. More likely, however, is that the child may not be fully cognizant of his emotions and problems. The behaviors may be his own private way of saying, "Somebody needs to step in here and give me a hand. To get your attention, Mom and Dad, I will behave in a disruptive way."

The parent team will need to take an in-depth look at the possibility of this behavior being a signal for help or intervention. If the parents decide that the behavior in question is indeed a signal, the behavior will still need to be dealt with. But the situation in the child's life that has caused the child to respond inappropriately with this behavior will also need to be thoroughly explored.

"Billy, your mother and I are concerned that you have been sent to the office at school again for skipping class. The last time you skipped that class we talked about the consequence. We decided that if you skipped class you would be choosing to work around the house all day

Saturday, or until you satisfactorily completed a list of chores. I am concerned that you have skipped again and chosen to do these chores all day Saturday. Let's go to Denny's for a snack so we can sit down and talk about this situation."

The meeting at the restaurant should not erase the consequence Billy has chosen. It should be a time when the parent must refrain from lectures and instead strain to listen to the child after asking open-ended questions. "What's going on in that class? Are you having a problem with the work or with any of your classmates?"

Billy may or may not be able to express his reasons for skipping that particular class. If there is a reason significant enough to cause him to have to work all day Saturday, the parent can at that point suggest alternative ways to handle the problem: going to the guidance counselor, asking to meet with the teacher after school, etc. The consequence should still stand, but Billy should also be listened to so that he knows his parents are concerned about the fact that he has chosen to do something that would necessitate this consequence.

Most of the time disruptive behavior is going to be found to be a signal for one thing: The child is testing the boundaries and the parents' authority. That is generally the natural reason for a child's behavioral problems. Signals must be looked for, but a parent needs to be careful not to use them as an excuse not to deal with the behavior in question.

5. *Do we as parents have this area of our lives under control?* Many times when parents talk to a counselor at the Sheridan House Counseling Center about their child's behavior, it is very evident to the therapist where the child learned the undesirable behavior. The parents might be concerned about the child's temper tantrums and verbal outbursts, and yet that is the very way they themselves respond to the challenges of life. When their child disobeys, they give him a very discourteous tongue lashing. Little wonder that this child grows up with a disrespectful mouth. It's as though he's saying, "My goal in life is to become an adult. Yelling and screaming must be an adult behavior since it is the way I see the significant adult in my life respond."

Before I can deal with an area I deem as deficient in my child's behavior, I must first see if he is learning it from me.

"Robey, your mother and I have made it a requirement for you to put your seat belt on every time you get into the car. You and I both know that this has been a hassle because we have had to tell you to do it most of the time. It occurs to me that I owe you an apology. I have told you to put the seat belt on when I don't do it myself. From now on, not only will I put on my own seat belt, but I will race to have it on before you do."

We would like to think that children hear with their ears. In reality they hear with their eyes. Children watch very carefully to see what the "adult" way to respond to life's situations are.

My father is a very neat and disciplined man. When we were children, my brother and I used to laugh at the way he kept his desk. Every paper clip and pencil was neatly stacked in its special place. It was so neat that he seemed to be able to tell if we just opened it up without touching anything. As children we talked about how ridiculous that kind of neatness was.

A few years ago my brother, Steve, and his family were visiting at my home. Steve and I were sitting at my desk. While we were talking he reached over, opened my desk drawer, and burst out laughing. "You keep your desk like Dad's, too." We laughed at the way we both have followed the pattern that he set for us—even though we used to laugh at it. He taught us well by setting a good example.

My wife has cross-stitched a poem that hangs in my office to help me remember this final point.

> A careful man I want to be,
> A little fellow follows me.
> I do not care to go astray,
> For fear he'll go the self-same way.
> I cannot once escape his eyes;
> What he sees me do, he tries.
> Like me, he says he's going to be
> That little chap that follows me.
> He thinks that I am big and fine;
> He believes in every word of mine.
> The base in me he must not see,
> That little chap that follows me.
> I must remember as I go
> Through summer sun and winter snow
> I'm building for the years to be,
> That little chap that follows me.
>
> —Author unknown

Summary

When the parenting team meets to discuss the children and their behavior, they will want to ask themselves these questions:

1. Is this behavior rebellious or simply childish?

2. Is this behavior of the nature that it will carry over into adulthood (will it have a lasting impact)?

3. Are we trying to control something that cannot be controlled?

4. Is this behavior a signal from our child?

5. Are we personally disciplined in this area? Do we set a good example for our child?

8

Drawing Up the Plan

LINDA AND EDDIE were sitting on their patio one Saturday morning as their children watched cartoons. "She is going to drive me crazy with this bedroom ordeal every Saturday," Linda exclaimed. "Every Saturday it is a major battle to get her to clean her room. Actually it would be easier to do it myself rather than go through all this."

Eddie and Linda were discussing their seven-year-old daughter, Barbie. It was supposed to be Barbie's job to clean her room and her closet every Saturday morning. Actually it had become a time when one of the parents had to stay in this little girl's bedroom with her to see that it got done. It was obviously time for a staff meeting.

The first question to be asked was, "Is Barbie's behavior and attitude about this job of cleaning her room just childishness or is it rebellion?" Eddie responded by saying that he thought it was obviously defiance and that it needed to be dealt with.

"Fine then," Linda said, almost crying. "You go in there next week and be the ogre who forces her to clean it."

"Linda, you sound like this is something that we should just overlook," Eddie responded.

This brought up *question number two*: Could this behavior have an impact on Barbie's adult life? "I think that if we don't deal with it now, she will continue to be rebellious as time goes on, and it will be more and more difficult to deal with her," Eddie said. He added that he thought neatness was a significant discipline for a child to understand. "Perhaps if she is continually required to clean her room and closet, she just might get to the point where she will decide to save herself some time by actually putting things back where they belong instead of letting them pile up."

Then came *question number three*: Were they trying to control something that they could not? On the surface it might have appeared that this was an issue that would always be a battle, but it could definitely be controlled. Their problem was that they were placing the responsibility for the cleaning of the room on the wrong shoulders. That became very obvious when Linda made the statement, "Fine then. You go in there next week and be the ogre who makes her clean her room."

Question number four concerned the signal the child's rebellious behavior was giving to the parents. It was little more than a child saying, "How important is this task to you, Mom? If I can make it difficult enough on you that you let me get out of it, I sure will continue to try and punish you each Saturday." The child was signaling what other children signal at her age: Rebellion.

The last thing that Eddie and Linda needed to look at was whether or not they themselves were disciplined in this area. Was a clean room something that Barbie would perceive as an adult behavior in her home? Did Eddie and Linda clean their room and set the example, or were they asking their child to do something that they themselves did not do?

At this point many parents might say, "Wait a minute. I have so many other things to do in the morning. I'm responsible for the whole family, not just my room. I clean my room later on in the day when everything has settled down." No one said it was easy to be a parent. But those little eyes are watching us. Their desire is to be just like we are. A parent must work overtime to perform the behavior that would be the right example for the children.

Developing the Plan

Once those questions had been dealt with, it was time to develop a plan of action. Eddie and Linda wanted to decide how they could handle this area of Barbie's life in a way that would be productive as well as instructive. How could they get Barbie to clean her room on Saturdays without all the fighting and bickering?

"It's not just her room that we are talking about here," Eddie said. "We also need a way to get her to do this chore without all the bickering."

Eddie was commenting on the reason for their difficulty with Barbie in this area. This little girl did not have the responsibility to clean her room on Saturdays. One of her parents was actually accepting that responsibility. Barbie might have been doing it with her hands, but her mother was standing over her, directing her. These parents were simply using their daughter's body to get the job done. Barbie had little else to do but think of how to argue with them. She certainly was not being left alone with the responsibility.

"How can we set up a plan that will place the responsibility on Barbie's shoulders rather than ours?" Eddie asked his wife.

They finally realized that they needed to give her the job and get out of the way. Together they decided to tell Barbie that from now on, it would be her job to clean her room and her closet before she watched any cartoons on Saturday.

The plan was to tell Barbie once this weekend and then explain it to her again on Friday, adding, "Barbie, when you think that this job is done, come and get one of us. We will need to inspect it before the television can be turned on."

"But my favorite cartoon is on at 9:00," Barbie complained. "What if I'm not done in time?"

"Let me say once again, Honey. You may not turn the cartoons on until we have inspected the room," Eddie said. "I would suggest that you start on the room the minute that you get up. It should only take you about twenty minutes. I have one other suggestion to make your job a little easier. Don't spend all week throwing your things on the closet floor. It will be easier for you on Saturday if you put things where they belong, as you go, during the week. But please understand that if you miss the first part of your cartoon show it will be your choice."

Did this work for them perfectly that next Saturday? Of course not. It took weeks before Barbie began to realize that the responsibility to clean the room in order to see the cartoons was on her shoulders. The one thing it did do immediately, however, was stop the parents from becoming the consequence. Lectures were no longer necessary. Barbie had no one to blame but herself if she spent an hour cleaning her room. There wasn't anyone else in the room to argue with.

Eddie and Linda found that they had to continue to meet to refine this new disciplinary program. Barbie got to the point the first few weeks that she was calling her parents back into the room every few minutes, saying that she was ready for them to inspect it. Finally her parents decided that they would come in and inspect only two times; after that they would only return every ten minutes. If Barbie called them in and she did not really have it ready, they would not be coming back in for ten more minutes. Very quickly Barbie learned that she was wasting her own time. She began to prepare for the inspections a little more seriously.

One thing was for sure, however. Neither parent felt like an ogre anymore. The responsibility for this chore was now resting on Barbie's shoulders where it belonged.

Paul and Diane were having problems with their twelve-year-old son, Michael, and his use of the telephone. Michael was spending hours each night on the phone. This often caused Paul to be unable to call home from his office. No matter how many times they had tried to explain to their son that it was inconsiderate to tie up the phone for so long, he continued this behavior. It finally got to the point where Paul was coming home in the evenings already furious at Michael because of the busy signals.

It was time for a staff meeting. This dad realized that the lectures were only making life miserable for everyone. At twelve, Michael was at an age where the father-son relationship was often strained anyway. The inappropriate way that the phone situation was being handled only caused further alienation between father and son. Paul had used himself and his yelling as the consequence for his son's selfish use of the phone.

Paul and Diane decided to go out for a cup of coffee to conduct a staff meeting. "What are we doing wrong?" this discouraged father asked his wife. "We are allowing this stupid phone problem to wreck our relationship with our son."

After taking time to calmly discuss the problem, they realized that they had never really established a consequence for inappropriate phone use. Paul had threatened that something would happen, but it never did—just one more lecture, followed by a threat that next time something would really happen.

"I just hate having to take away his phone privileges. I don't want to alienate him from his friends," Paul said. "I guess that's why I have never done anything about it."

"Unfortunately," Diane replied, "our threats have served to alienate our son from us."

In this calm setting these parents realized that they would have to place the responsibility back on Michael's shoulders. It was decided that Michael would be told that he could use the phone for twenty minutes anytime between seven and eight in the evening. He was to time his own calls. If he went over the allotted time, he would be choosing to go without using the phone for the next forty-eight hours. If, however, he followed this rule for the next two weeks, his time would be expanded to thirty minutes.

Once this was accomplished, the responsibility was placed back on Michael's shoulders. There was no more need for a lecture. This young person would be placed in a position of having to learn about making his own decisions. Paul now had a logical way to handle the problem that would not cause him constant frustration. He was no longer placed in a position of being the enemy. In the past Michael had spent his time on the telephone looking over his shoulder to see if his parents were coming to tell him to get off the phone. Now, under the new plan, he spent his phone time looking at the clock. He was forced to deal with the time rather than a screaming dad.

It is not the purpose of this chapter to suggest specific consequences for inappropriate behavior. Consequences may vary from one family to the next. The significant factor here is that parents hold staff meetings to establish a plan.

There is one other reason for the staff meeting: It helps both parents work together on the problem so that they will be together on the solution. When each parent handles inappropriate behavior in a different way, the child will quickly learn that it is not the behavior that he must deal with. Rather it is the parent in charge at the time that he has to deal with. "When my dad tells me to get up in the morning, I know that I had better do it. My mom, however, is a different story. She'll come back into my room a half-dozen times."

Strive for Consistency

A football team goes into a huddle before each play to make sure all the players are coordinated in their effort. Otherwise, the quarterback might be looking for his receiver to go long in order to catch a pass while the receiver decides to act on his own and block. The fact that they are not working together, consistently following the game plan, means this team is not going to succeed. The same is true for the family that is not consistently working together.

To strive for a consistent plan means that the two parents may need to compromise with each other. Spouses won't always agree at first about how to handle the behavioral problem. They will need to keep talking at the staff meeting until they can agree upon a plan that will be beneficial for the child's development. By compromising, the plan will be one that both parents can uphold.

The fact that the parents are together in their approach is perhaps more important than the plan itself. It is very unhealthy for children to see their parents divided over how to handle them. It can often place them in a position of guilt because their parents are fighting over them. Despite that guilt, though, a child will still try to divide the parents to get his own way. Wise parents will stay in the staff meeting until they can decide upon a way to handle a behavior that satisfies both spouses.

Freddy was sixteen and had had his license for six months. His parents let him use the car to go to school functions, but he was constantly late in returning home. His parents, Jack and Gladys, found that the lectures about responsibility weren't working. Neither were the threats. They went out for a staff meeting.

"Gladys, I've had it with the way he's handling the car. If Freddy is late one more time, I'm going to take it away until he turns seventeen," Jack said.

"That might be a little harsh," Gladys responded. "We don't want to go overboard."

"Overboard," Jack almost screamed. "You think we are asking too much to require him to be home with the car on time? Whose side are you on anyway?"

"There are no sides in this issue," Gladys said. "I agree with you 100 percent. Something must be done about Freddy's lack of respect for his curfew. I just think that taking the car away for the rest of the year won't teach him anything."

Jack and Gladys stayed at the restaurant for several hours discussing the purpose and the opportunity they had in this situation. The car was very important to their son, and they could use it as a tool to teach Freddy about punctuality. If he was late, they compromised by taking the car away for a week and then giving it back. When Freddy was late again, they decided to take it away again for a week. Freddy would eventually learn that it was his fault that he kept losing the car for one week at a time.

At the start of this meeting, Jack and Gladys had been at opposite ends of the pole as far as a plan of action was concerned. But they were willing to stay in that staff meeting long enough for the parent who was the most frustrated to blow off steam. Then they were able to work out a solution that would teach a lesson rather than just completely deny the child an opportunity—not only an opportunity to use the car, but also an opportunity to fail and to accept the consequences of that failure.

It is important that parents work toward a plan that both spouses are willing to uphold. Compromise will often be necessary because consistency is mandatory.

It may seem to many parents that this idea of a parental staff meeting is new. After all, I don't remember my parents or grandparents announcing that they were going out for a cup of coffee to have a family staff meeting. Perhaps they didn't call it that. But they had the meetings just the same. In centuries past parents sat on the front porch and spent hours discussing the family. Parents of the past were less distracted by interruptions such as television, telephones, and evening meetings away from the house. It came natural to the parent of the past to end each day sitting and talking for hours.

Today's parents often try to communicate by writing quick notes to each other on the kitchen blackboard or on a magnetized pad stuck to the refrigerator. It is because of today's hectic lifestyles and distractions that the important things of life must be scheduled. Since staff meetings don't happen as part of the natural flow of a parent's life anymore, they must now be formally scheduled.

A Planned Response

When my daughter was only eleven months old, I came home one afternoon to review some files. As I walked in the front door, I heard my wife scream. Racing into the nursery, I found her holding our baby as the infant was having a seizure. I ran to the phone, called the doctor, and he instructed me to get to the hospital immediately.

I was so distraught that I did exactly what the doctor told me to. I ran out to the car, got in, and started for the hospital—without my wife and child! When I realized what I had done, I turned around and found my wife, holding our daughter, waiting for me in the driveway.

When we got to the hospital, I was in such a state that I almost needed medical assistance myself. When my daughter was taken care of and back to normal, I asked the doctor if I could talk to him. "Is this going to happen again?" I asked. He told me that it was possible that my daughter might have another seizure because that was the way she responded to high fevers. "Then you've got to help me," I said. "I didn't respond to this too well. I had no idea what to do, so I went crazy! Tell me what to do in case it happens again."

We spent quite awhile talking about what to do and how to handle my daughter if another seizure should occur. He helped me work out a plan so I would feel a little more confident in my ability to care for my child.

Sure enough, a month later, Torrey had a second seizure. And because I had a plan of action, this time I didn't panic. Of course, I didn't enjoy dealing with the situation; but at least I was able to respond effectively and with confidence.

The same can be said where discipline is concerned. Parents wish that they didn't have to deal with it, but they do. And when they have a good plan of action to work from, there is less chance of overreaction. Staff meetings will help everyone stay calm, and this will ultimately help the child. Plan to have staff meetings so you can plan for the child's growth.

Summary

1. Staff meetings relieve parental frustrations because you realize you finally have a plan.

2. Staff meetings help both parents work together toward a consistent plan.

3. Staff meetings should be used as a time to review the plan to see if alterations need to be made.

9

"Allow My Child to Fail?"

"YOU SOUND AS if I should set up a plan and then get out of the way and watch my child fail," a parent said to me after a seminar. "How can I do that? I don't want him to fail."

No parent does. But keep in mind that it's the long-term goal of the discipline process that counts. The parent could attempt to set up an environment for the child that would be failure-free. "If I remove all the untouchable items within my infant's grasp, then I won't have to say no." But that kind of philosophy only meets the needs of the parent and postpones teaching the appropriate response to the word no.

Yes, children are going to fail. It is not our job as parents to cover all their failures while they grow up. Parents are to provide a home environment that is consistent and that they understand. Then when our children fail, we are to be there with a plan that will help them learn two things: First, that there are consequences in life for irresponsible behavior or for violations of authority; and second, that it is possible to bounce back after they do fail.

Many children have never had the opportunity to learn how to deal with failure. I recently had such a person in my office. He was no longer a child, however. He was a thirty-year-old man.

"I don't know how to deal with failure," he was crying. "When I was younger, my mother would give me things to do or tell me not to do other things. If I failed or disobeyed, she would always cover for me."

This man went on to say how his mother would always say things like, "That's okay, Jimmy, but next time you do that . . ." He never really tasted the consequences of failure, nor did he have an opportunity to learn to deal with it. His mother had always rescued him. Once she had badgered him about completing a school science project that was due the next day. When he failed to get it done, she stayed up all night finishing it for him. He got a good grade on that childhood project; but he was not getting very good "grades" in his adult life. He had recently lost his job because Mom was no longer around to buffer him from failure.

Part of disciplining children is setting the boundaries and then getting out of the way. Does that mean that parents should let their children fail at the science projects of the world? Yes, I believe it does. As parents we should do everything in our power to offer assistance—and then get out of the way.

When my son learned to ride his two-wheel bicycle, it was a painful experience (more painful for me than it was for Robey). The day came when it was time to take off the training wheels. That afternoon I ran along behind him, holding on to the back of his seat. I was not going to let him go through the pain of falling off his bike. I believe that if I were in better physical condition, I would have run along holding on to that seat indefinitely. But he would not have learned anything. To master the discipline of balance and coordination necessary to ride a two-wheel bicycle meant that Dad had to let go.

This was a difficult decision. His little face kept looking back to see if I was still holding on. I knew that this decision would mean that he probably would get hurt and skin his knees. I also knew that if he were ever going to have any fun bicycling, I had to let go.

If I were only interested in meeting my needs, I would have made the decision to either hold on to the bicycle forever or put the training wheels back on. Perhaps I would have said, "Forget it, Robey. You don't need to learn how to ride a bike." I had to allow him to fail so that he could learn.

Stepping Back

The disciplinary process means that we have to get out of the way and go through the pain of allowing children to fail. I wish we could make it so they never had to face failure, but that is not possible in this world. A significant lesson to have learned by the time a child becomes an adult is not only how to avoid failure, but also how to deal with it when it happens.

I would rather have my children fail—and learn to handle that failure—while they are living in the loving environment of our home. Some homes today attempt to set up an environment that protects their child from failure. By doing this, however, they also prevent that child from learning how to bounce back after that failure. When this child leaves home and arrives on the college campus, he begins to face personal failure for the first time. Mom is no longer there to buffer his personal relationships or responsibilities. At this late stage in life, he is in a lonely dormitory or apartment rather than with his loving family.

Connie was a girl who had grown up in a Christian home. She was an only child and her parents loved her very much. They made a mistake while raising her, however, by smothering her to the point of trying to keep failure from her path.

There were many times while she was a child or adolescent that she had decisions to make. These decisions might have been of a rather minor nature: when to clean her room, when to do homework, which courses to take, which friends to go out with. It didn't matter what the decisions were. Connie's parents thought they were helping by making the decisions for her. After all, they thought they were relieving her of the pressure of deciding. Actually these parents were trying to avoid the embarrassment of accepting their daughter's failure. It was just easier to decide everything for her. It took less time and less discussion.

Unfortunately, the fact that Connie had grown up in an environment where she was not allowed any decisions meant that she was very immature in the decision-making process. She was also totally unfamiliar with consequences for poor decisions or personal irresponsibility. In other words, she was not prepared to leave home, even though it was time to go away to college.

Once away from home, Connie very quickly met with disaster. This girl was in my office because she had made some very serious mistakes that had caused her to completely fall apart. As a result, Connie felt that it would be impossible to ever go back home to parents who had unintentionally taught her that they could not accept her failures. Something inside Connie told her she should not return to the nest and allow her parents to once again take over. Instead, she began the agonizing process of learning how to decide things for herself as she dealt with failure for the first time—an experience that should have taken place years before.

It is very difficult to watch our children fail, but the circumstances that cause them to fail when they are children will not have a lasting effect. On the other hand, many of the things that adults fail at will impact them for a lifetime. If Johnny is allowed to fail at the handling of his money or his homework when he is a child, it may cause him some difficulty. This failure will not have as lasting an effect, however, as it would if he mishandled his money or work when he becomes an adult.

Learning from Failure

Difficult as it is, parents must allow these failures to happen and then be there to pick up the pieces. Experiencing failure as a child causes less severe damage than facing failures for the first time as an adult.

"Time and time again I told him to work on his science project," a parent told me. "I finally decided to get off his back and let him deal with the consequences." Her son waited until the last minute and then had to turn in a project that was below his potential because he did not have time to do it properly. The mother was embarrassed—but not nearly as embarrassed as her son. He received a very poor grade.

"What did you learn from this experience, Billy?" This parent was quick to take advantage of this failure. She wanted to allow her child the opportunity to think about the reasons for his failure and how it made him feel. It was a very valuable time in the child's development.

Allowing a child to fail really means allowing that child the opportunity to make decisions. When parents try to remove all possibility of failure from a child's life, they also remove all opportunity for the child to learn decision making. We have all heard parents say, "I sure wish my child would learn how to make better decisions."

My response to that parent would be, "Has your child had the opportunity to practice making any decisions for himself?" Decision-making skills must be learned, and the only way they can be learned is if they are taught.

Set up the boundaries and let your children make decisions within those boundaries. So often parents make every single imaginable decision for their children. "I only do it because he makes such horrible choices." As a parent I would rather have my child deal with some of those poor choices now than later.

Let children fail at little things early in life. One parent told me how she argued about absolutely everything with her ten-year-old daughter. "We even argue about what she is going to wear to church on Sunday evening!"

"Well, let's start with that one," I said to her. "Have you given her any choices in the matter of clothes for Sunday evening church, or do you make all those decisions for her?"

"I have to decide them for her," this mother responded with exasperation. "If I didn't, she would wear totally inappropriate outfits. Would you want me to let her wear shorts to church?"

"No," I responded, "then you would be going from one extreme to the other—from boundaries that are too rigid so as to avoid failure to a system with no boundaries at all. Your daughter is at an age where you need to widen the parameters of the boundaries. Allow her some room for decisions and failure."

We talked about how this mother could show her daughter all the outfits that would be appropriate for a ten-year-old to wear to Sunday night church. We also talked about the fact that a ten-year-old should be able to wear less formal clothes than would be appropriate for an adult.

"Once you have made her aware of the various outfits that would be acceptable, then it is time to get out of the way and let her decide for herself," I advised.

The next time I saw that mother I asked how her little experiment was going. She told me that the system was working well, that there were no more arguments, and her daughter was choosing her own clothes.

As I listened, I sensed that she was not totally satisfied, and I asked her why.

"She chooses things from that group I have labeled as appropriate, but it's the combinations of those clothes that are killing me," this mother responded. "They don't go well together, and I have the hardest time not sending her back into her room again. I'm allowing her that privilege, though, even if it kills me."

This little girl was not her mother's baby doll, to be dressed up and shown off. This was a little girl who needed the opportunity to decide and the opportunity to choose to fail. Children need to begin learning how to deal with these two areas some time in life. What better place than at home? Don't avoid failure and the decision-making process that goes with it. Allow it, nurture it, and then help them learn from it.

Summary

1. Children need the opportunity to learn how to handle failure.

2. Parents must establish a plan and then get out of the way, allowing the children the opportunity to succeed or fail, to be responsible or irresponsible, and then to handle the consequences.

3. Having the privilege to fail means a child has been given the privilege to make some decisions. Learning to make decisions is a concept that is best practiced in the shelter of one's childhood.

10

"What Do I Do about Lying?"

"HIS CONSTANT LYING is driving me crazy!" This is not an unusual comment to hear from a parent of a seven- or eight-year-old. Parents always want to know why their child doesn't tell the truth, and perhaps that is the perfect way to begin dealing with the problem of lying.

Parents must be willing to become students of their children. They need to study them like a top salesperson sizes up a prospect. The salesperson wants to know what makes the prospective buyer tick, why he or she says certain things. By studying these things, the salesperson begins to understand the person he is talking to. Not only that, but it also helps him make the sale.

Several years ago I was in the home of a friend who was not a Christian. There was a knock at the door and, as he responded to the knock, three people from a local church entered to talk with him. I was excited to be able to be there and listen to them tell my friend about their faith. Their mission in that house was similar to mine. They were interested in leading him to Christ.

As these three people began to talk, I began to get discouraged with their approach. They had not come to study my friend. They had not come into his home to listen and get to know him or to find out anything about him. They had come into his home to say what they had to say and leave. As my friend tried to talk, they interrupted. Consequently they failed at their mission.

When our children are involved in any behavior that is contrary to the boundaries we have set for them, it is important to study them so as to be able to appraise what it is that their behavior is saying to us.

Lying Due to Low Self-Esteem

Johnny was a boy who was constantly bragging about all the things that he had and what he could do. "Last week my dad took me to play baseball at our church picnic, and I hit a home run every time I got up to bat." He exaggerated about his own personal achievements, and he fell into the lying trap of continually boasting, "I'm better than you."

Billy came up to Johnny in school one day and said, "Did you see the new car in my driveway? My dad just bought a four-wheel-drive truck that can go up the side of mountains." Johnny responded with, "That's nothing. My dad has two four-wheel-drive trucks that can . . . ."

Billy, in his frustration of constantly having Johnny respond with wild lies like this, interrupted, "Oh yeah, where are these two trucks? How come I've never seen them?" At that point Johnny created an even wilder story. "They are at our house in the mountains. You've never seen them because you've never been to our house in the mountains. When we are there my dad lets me drive one of them."

Later Johnny was forced to face his lies when Billy saw him in his yard with his mom. Billy said, "Mrs. Smith, Johnny says that you have a home in the mountains with two four-wheel-drive trucks. Is that true?" Mrs. Smith was shocked, but she was used to what she had considered to be Johnny's overactive imagination.

Her question at this point was how to handle this situation. Billy was obviously gloating at the fact that he had trapped her son. The other area to be analyzed was why her son persisted at telling these lies.

"Billy, let me talk to Johnny for a moment. We'll come over to talk to you later." Mrs. Smith looked at her son and said, "Johnny, you need to sit down on the porch here so that we can talk."

She began by letting her son know that lying or exaggerating was not acceptable and that it was obviously a problem area for Johnny. "Son, we all have areas of our lives that we have to work on. Telling the truth, the whole truth, is an area that you will have to work on."

Johnny cut in with, "Well, we keep talking about having a cabin some day, and in the summer we go up to a cabin and stay for a week."

"That is correct, Johnny," the boy's mom responded. "But that's a far cry from what you told Billy, isn't it?"

"It's almost the same, Mom."

Mrs. Smith continued to calmly correct her child, trying to help him distinguish the truth from the fiction. "It's not at all the same, Honey. We don't own a cabin, and we don't own a four-wheel-drive truck."

"Well, I guess I exaggerated a little, but thanks for not saying it in front of Billy."

Johnny's mom then looked him straight in the eyes and said, "We are going to have to correct those statements that you made, Son. We are going to go over to Billy's house, and you will have to say that you are sorry that you lied. You will have to tell him that we don't have a cabin nor do we have a four-wheel-drive truck."

Johnny burst into tears, "Oh, Mom, please don't make me do that! I can't!"

Mrs. Smith had finally decided to take a stand on what she had previously considered to be Johnny's imaginative stories. After further talk the child realized that he had no option. Mother and child went over to the friend's house and Johnny apologized. Johnny didn't look the friend right in the eye and do it the way it could have been done. He said the words that were necessary, however, and was very humiliated.

On the way back home, Mrs. Smith then had the opportunity to give the child some positive comments. "I'm not happy about the fact that you lied, Johnny. I am very proud about the way you have now handled the apology, however."

"Well you made me do it, Mom," Johnny said through his tears. To this his mother responded, "That's right; but you still did it, and I'm proud to have a son who accepts the consequences for his behavior."

Johnny's mom went on to say, "Let me say one more thing. The next time you tell someone something that is not true—and I hope there won't be a next time—we will do the same thing. I love you; please don't make me do this again."

The handling of this behavior was only half over, however. It was now time to study the situation. Mother and father needed to set time aside to talk about why they thought their child would tell such exaggerated stories.

Usually parents can boil the reasoning down to a feeling of inadequacy. Children often feel like they don't have anything positive going for themselves, so they have to invent something.

Johnny may have felt that he didn't have any friends because he wasn't good at anything, or that he didn't possess anything that other children his age would think was "cool."

The reality of Johnny's reasoning was that he didn't have any friends because his constant lies made him obnoxious to be around. He was his own worst enemy in this vicious circle. The fewer friends he had, the more lies he told to get people to like him.

As Mom and Dad studied their child's lying and low self-esteem, they decided upon a two-fold plan. First, they decided they would continue with the plan of forcing him to face the people he lied to and that Dad would reinforce that plan.

Second, these parents decided that Dad needed to set aside a specific amount of time each week to be with their son. If this constant lying was a signal that Johnny was lonely and felt valueless, Dad would help work on that problem. The time they spent together would be devoted to practicing sports, but it would also be a time when father and son would just be together.

Dad also would be with Johnny at bedtime each night. After helping Johnny with his prayers, this father decided he would stay in the boy's room for fifteen more minutes and lie down on the bed with his son, talking softly, or just relaxing together. It would be a time for Dad to reinforce to his son that "Johnny is special."

With this plan, the parents were able to deal with the behavior and establish a plan that would help the child feel better about himself so that he did not need to lie. A plan like this takes discipline on the parts of all parties involved. When he realized he faced the same consequence every time, Johnny would eventually learn to discipline himself to resist the temptation to lie. Mom and Dad would have to discipline themselves, too, to apply the same consequence every time. And they had to discipline their schedules to spend more one-on-one time with their child. The things that count in life always require our time.

Lying to Avoid a Consequence

What about the lie that signals little more than, "I don't want to get caught"? Those are often the most frustrating lies to deal with. The child has violated a preestablished rule, but when confronted with it, he denies any involvement.

After a hard day at work, Jack returned home to find that a catastrophe had taken place. When he entered the front door, he found a lamp overturned and broken in the living room. His two boys were both in their bedrooms, and Jack's wife, Doris, was in the kitchen, very upset.

"I see we have a problem," Jack said as he attempted to comfort his wife. This husband was surprised as he noticed that his wife was fighting back the tears. "We can replace the lamp right away, Honey," Jack said.

"Oh, it's not the lamp that gets me down. It's their constant lying that wears me out," Doris responded. "I was outside in the frontyard talking to a neighbor when I heard the crash. When I came in I found one of their toy airplanes next to the lamp. I don't know how many times I have told them both not to play with the airplanes in the living room. As I looked around the room, there was nothing else to be found. Whoever did this vanished immediately. I called them both into the room, and one claimed that he was immersed in his homework when it happened. The other said that he was in the bathroom at the time. Neither one of them claimed to know anything about it."

There are a few things to be noted from this conversation. Doris claimed that she was constantly telling the boys not to do something. This indicates to us that she had threatened, pleaded, or lectured, but never held them accountable. She had told them not to play with their planes in the living room, but when they did, she never had a consequence that would teach them not to do it again.

These two children had also learned another unacceptable behavior. If they lied and stuck to their story, they would eventually be able to escape responsibility. After a few moments of asking questions, the parents would say, "Okay this time, but if you do it again, we will get to the bottom of this." The children soon learned the lesson of deceptive perseverance. "Just hold out and Mom and Dad will get busy doing other things."

The biggest problem with this lack of parenting is what it does to the relationship. Soon the parents find it difficult to like their child. They still love the child, they just don't like him.

Jack decided that particular day was the day to start dealing with this irresponsible behavior. He went into the bedrooms and asked both of the boys to come and sit in the living room. "Boys," this father began, "we have a very serious problem here, and it has very little to do with the lamp." Jack remained calm as he talked with his sons. "Someone has broken this lamp and is unwilling to admit to their behavior," he said. Immediately both boys began denying any knowledge of the incident.

"It's not the lamp that worries me," Jack began again. "The consequence for playing with the plane in the living room and destroying the lamp is only money. The more serious matter is the fact that the person who did it is now lying. The consequence for doing this is much more serious. We are going to sit here until the one who did it admits to it."

Almost immediately the boys were asking to talk to their father and explain how they were sure that the other boy had broken the lamp.

This saddened Jack as he saw how out-of-hand the lying had become. "We are not here to be detectives and tattle on each other. I don't want you to tell me about what the other person has done. I want the one who did it to admit to his mistake and accept the consequences," he said.

"It's not fair," the older boy was quick to say. "Why should we both have to sit here if just one of us did it?"

"You are exactly right, Billy," the father agreed. "It isn't fair that we all have to sit here, myself included. Neither is it fair that the lamp is broken and that we have to use money that was going to be spent elsewhere, on the purchase of a new lamp. There are a lot of things that aren't fair in this situation. The most unfair thing, however, is that members of this family would violate our trust in each other by not telling the truth. We are going to sit here and talk about this until the one who did it can admit to it."

It was a drastic measure. The fact that it was a Wednesday night and the family had planned to go to church meant that those plans had to be changed. As they sat there, the boys realized that their father was serious; they were going to sit there until the problem of lying was resolved. The boys were learning that their father now took lying as a very serious offense to the family.

Bedtime rolled around and Jack had to make some decisions. Should they go to bed without resolving the issue? What about school the next day? Jack decided to send them off to bed and to school the next morning. But he told them that they would be right back in those seats after school.

The next afternoon the boys began to realize that their father was indeed serious. Before bedtime that second day, the older son asked if he could speak with his father alone. At that point he burst into tears and confessed his lie. Jack gave his son a hug and told him that he loved him. This father reaffirmed that he would never like the fact that the boy had lied but that he would always love him.

At that point Jack told his son what the consequence would be. First, the boy would have to go back into the living room and apologize to the family for lying and causing everyone to have to sit for so long. Then the boy was told that he would have to do his brother's chores for him on Saturday because he had caused him to have to sit there. The consequence for breaking the lamp was that he would have to pay for it out of his allowance. The consequence for lying would be some extra work around the house for a week.

"If you had told the truth in the first place, this would have only cost you money. I hope that you have learned from this mistake. If there is another lie, we will do the same thing. We will stop everything until the truth comes out," Jack said.

That night Jack sat for a while on the side of the beds of both his boys, not to lecture them further but to reassure them of his love.

Two weeks later a similar situation happened, and once again a lie was told. "Boys, it's time for us to go sit in the living room," Doris said to her boys. "You know what happened last time the truth was not told." Almost immediately the boy who was lying spoke up and said, "I did it, Mom."

It was going to take them awhile to respond with the truth immediately after they were asked. They were learning, however. They were learning because Jack and Doris were committed to teach their children the importance of honesty.

This was also a time for these two parents to see to it that they were setting an example of honesty. Very quickly Jack found that he was a hypocrite when it came to teaching this lesson.

One evening a short time after the incident with the lamp, the younger boy had been caught doing something dishonest at school. After Doris called Jack at the office, he decided that when he got home that night he would take his son for a ride and talk about the incident.

As this father and son rode together that evening, Jack talked to his son about the importance of honesty. Jack went on to say that rules were established for our good and that they had to be followed. As Jack continued his talk about honesty, he reached over to turn on his radar detector.

Instantly both he and his son realized the hypocrisy of this action. "What do you think about me using this radar detector, Son? Do you think that it is honest for me to try to use it to break the law?"

He and his son talked about it, and when they pulled in the driveway at home, Jack called the rest of his family into the garage. "I've been dishonest and a poor example for my family by using this radar detector. I'm sorry and I ask your forgiveness." With that Jack smashed the radar detector and threw it in the garbage. "Boys, this work that we are doing on honesty and telling the truth has helped me be a better person. Thank you," he said.

Sound a bit dramatic? It might have been, but it was an event that those boys will never forget. They got to see their dad stand up for honesty even if it cost him. Those boys got to view responsible adult behavior at its best.

Lying is a serious behavior that must be dealt with in a serious manner. When it is excused or left unchecked, it can become a very divisive power within a family. It takes time to teach this lesson, but it's time well invested.

Summary

1. When your child lies about something, study the incident to see if it is a signal that (1) he is showing how inadequate he feels, or (2) he is attempting to avoid a consequence.

2. Deal with the lying behavior by using a consequence; but deal with the child by reassuring him that you care about who he is as a person.

3. Dealing with lies takes time and a consistent plan.

4. The children need to know that lying is a very serious offense in your family.

5. Evaluate your own life to see that you are setting an example of responsible adult behavior.

PART III

Spanking:
Why and How

11

Why Spank?

I HAD THE PRIVILEGE of going to college and graduate school in the 1960s and 1970s. During that period corporal punishment was looked upon as barbaric and out of touch with the times. Though I was a Christian, I adopted the platform of my secular education. I, too, felt that all spanking was abusive.

The year 1974 brought a major turn in my professional direction. Prior to that time I had been employed by the state of Florida as a counselor for delinquent children. In April of that year I was called to the position of director of Sheridan House for Boys.

Sheridan House was, at that time, a ministry offering residential care to adolescent boys who needed to be removed from their homes because of disciplinary problems. Today it has grown to the point that it offers many additional ministries.

During my first two weeks as director of Sheridan House, I put my books neatly on the shelves and hung my diplomas in a strategic location so everyone would know I was well qualified.

At my first meeting with the staff, I announced that the behavioral problems would all be handled through counseling and group therapy. At the end of those first two weeks all the residential staff resigned.

I now found myself in a new position. No longer could I pass down edicts to other people who were living with the children. From that day until we were able to find new staff members, I became a houseparent. I actually had to work with the children firsthand.

It's Your Move

I didn't realize it at the time, but that was God's training for me. One of the first nights that I was left alone with the boys, I ran into difficulty with my "utopian" plan for discipline. I remember walking out of my office into the big living room at 8:30 P.M. Twelve boys were there, watching television or playing games. With all the authority I could muster, I announced, "At 9:00 I want the television turned off and everyone in bed."

There was no response, but that didn't matter since I knew they had heard me; so I walked back into my office. Forty-five minutes later, at 9:15, I noticed that I could still hear the television. Obviously they had gone to bed and someone had neglected to turn it off.

Walking back into the room, I was shocked to find out that no one had budged. I stepped in front of the television and once again announced that it was time for bed. All the boys stopped what they were doing and started for bed. All the boys, that is, but one! A little fellow named Al sat in his seat and attempted to watch television around me. I turned the set off and said to him, "Al, it's time for bed." He just sat there waiting for me to move so that he could turn the television back on.

At that point I heard myself make a statement that forced a turning point in my life. "Al, if you don't get up and go to bed immediately, you will be forcing me to spank you."

I could not believe I had said that. Where did that statement come from? As soon as it was out of my mouth, I wished I could have it back. Al looked at me as if to say, "It's your move."

Not knowing what to do, but realizing that the authority and safety of this home were on the line, I escorted him by the arm into my office. I repeated that it was my job to spank him since he had disobeyed and had basically asked me to do it. I told him that I was not going to chase him around the room but that he needed to submit to my leadership.

Three hours later Al gave in and bent over a chair. With tears in my eyes I spanked him on the bottom with a paddle that had been left by the previous director. After accepting his spanking, Al slumped down on the couch, and I could see that all the fight and arrogance had gone out of him. Not knowing what else to do, I sat down next to him and we talked.

I explained to him how we had gotten to that point because he had rebelled against my leadership. I told him that I was committed to caring about him—even during the difficult times. "Al, please don't make me do this again. But please understand, I care about you enough to do it if you refuse to do what you are told." I gave him a hug and walked him to bed.

That night it was impossible for me to sleep. I realized the need to establish order, and yet all my training had led me to believe that I had just abused a child.

The next morning was filled with even more confusion. At 5:30 A.M. I walked into the boys' rooms to wake them up. When I walked into Al's room, to my horror I found that he was not there. Had he run away during the night? In deep despair, I walked into the kitchen, trying to decide what to do next. There, to my shock, was Al.

He had gotten out of bed early and set the table for me. He was so pleasant I might have thought he was a different child in Al's body. It was the first time I had seen him attempt a smile. This was ridiculous! Had the spanking rendered this child senseless?

Breakfast was the best time I'd had with the boys in the three weeks I had been there. They laughed and joked freely, and to my surprise Al was going out of his way to be helpful. It was obvious that the children felt safe and protected, that someone other than a child was in control. After breakfast and devotions, I took the children to school and returned to Sheridan House, confused.

Later that morning as I sat in my office, the "Cookie Lady" came for her weekly visit. This was a lady named Molly Sipple who baked cookies for the children. Mrs. Sipple was in her seventies and probably did not have a lot of education, certainly not as much education as I had, anyway.

As Mrs. Sipple walked into my office, she was quick to notice that I was suffering. Sitting there after a night with no sleep, it was not difficult to surmise that I was having trouble!

"Is everything okay, Bob?" she asked me. I was quick to let her know that I had everything under control. As a way of changing the subject, Mrs. Sipple looked around my office and noticed all my books. "Wow, that sure is a lot of books," she commented. "Which of these books do you think is the most significant as far as the family is concerned?" she asked.

Finally a situation I could handle! I was ready for a question like this. "Well, Mrs. Sipple, there are several." At that point I listed a half-dozen classical books on childhood development, knowing that she would have never heard of any of them.

After I finished my sophisticated list, she looked me straight in the eye and asked, "What about the Bible, Bob?" Quickly I attempted to recover. "Oh, of course, didn't I mention that?" It was too late, however. She had caught me.

At that point I told her about the incident of the previous night—and Mrs. Sipple began to teach. She reached over, brushed the dust off of my Bible, and opened it to Proverbs.

That morning God used this lady to give me a cram course on children and discipline. "He who spares his rod hates his son, But he who loves him disciplines him promptly" (Prov. 13:24, NKJV). There are several lessons about children and corporal punishment in that verse. The first is the assumption that children will require spanking as a form of correction.

Spanking, handled correctly, is a very difficult thing to do. It often causes the parent more heartache than it does the child. Proverbs 13:24 indicates that if you love the child, however, you will respond to his needs by punishing him this way.

When my first child turned five, it was time to take her in for her booster shot. I didn't anticipate how difficult this decision was going to be. When it got right down to it and we were in the doctor's office, Torrey looked up at me and said, "Don't let him do this to me, Daddy."

My first thought was to say, "Okay, you're right. We don't need to go through this agony. Let's forget the shot and get out of here." However, that would have been meeting my need to avoid an unpleasant duty. It would certainly not have met the needs of my child. Torrey needed that booster shot for the sake of her health. I want her to like me, though, and that tempts me to say that she doesn't have to do anything she doesn't want to. But I am the one responsible for her growth and well-being. I am the one responsible to see to it that she gets the things she needs in life—though, not necessarily all the things she wants.

The pediatrician said the booster shot was necessary, so I saw to it that Torrey received it. The same is true for spanking. Just as I trust the pediatrician to help me protect Torrey's physical health and well-being, I need to trust God with even more faith that He knows about *all* my child's needs.

God's Prescription for Discipline

Why is spanking the correct approach for a child's rebellious behavior? Primarily because it is God's prescription. After he had been spanked, Al's change in attitude was amazing. It was as if he knew that he had been punished and forgiven, and now the slate was clean. He was able to go on about his life, for a while, with a clean slate.

The second part of that verse encourages parents to "be prompt to punish him." Many forms of punishment are available. Most do not take place in a very quick manner, however. Going to bed early is one possibility, but usually it is not prompt. The child may spend the rest of the day with that hanging over him. Such punishment might be instructive when the problem is not one of rebellion. But rebellion must be handled differently. Telling a child that he will be going to bed early for his defiance will only cause him to be more defiant as the day goes on. Rebellion should be dealt with immediately. Spanking makes it possible for the consequence to be administered and the relationship to be healed.

In reality, rebellion is a relationship problem. The child refuses to accept the leadership and authority of the parent. "I won't do it," he says, or, "I will do whatever I choose to do." Those are typical statements that rebellious behavior is signaling. They must be dealt with promptly and objectively so that the parent and child can get on with their relationship.

Al was told that whether he was spanked again or not was up to him. If he acted in such a way as to rebel, he would be choosing to be spanked. That one spanking was not his last. Nor was his rebellious attitude so easily changed the next time. Eventually, after a long period of understanding that we were committed to love him through both the good and the bad times, his life turned around.

Not long ago Al came back to visit Sheridan House. He is now a productive adult in our community, and he came to us with his thirteen-year-old nephew. "My nephew is running around in the streets and needs help," Al said. "He doesn't think that anybody cares, and I told him I knew that you would care since you had cared enough about me to stop me from ruining my life."

Spanking gets the consequence over quickly. Spanking lets a child know that there is a line that he may not go over without suffering prompt consequences. It forces a child to learn to discipline himself.

"He who spares the rod, hates his son. . . ." The instructions couldn't be plainer than that. We have heard the experts of the 1960s; parents have tried the plans of those experts and found they don't work. We easily accepted their instructions not to spank because spanking is so difficult to do. It breaks a parent's heart to spank a little child. But "he who loves him . . ." will be prompt to see that all the things that are necessary become part of his life. That includes booster shots, vegetables, and spankings when they are called for. God has instructed it because He knows the rebellious nature of the child. God has instructed it because He knows the marshmallow nature of the parent. The job of parenting is not easy; but it is mandatory.

Summary

1. God requires spanking only for rebellious behavior.

2. Spanking is the proper consequence for rebellious behavior for two reasons: (1) God says it is, and (2) It quickly takes care of the relationship problem that rebellion represents.

3. Spanking should be handled in a prompt manner.

Warning. Spanking can be abused. Please read the next chapter for important information on how to spank.

12

The Proper Way to Spank

IN CHAPTER 6 I told of the time when Robey, in his Superman pajamas, got out of bed after being told not to. It was one of those situations where he was directly defying his parent, and yet he looked so cute while he was doing it.

There are many decisions in life that require personal parental discipline. I had told him he would be spanked for his disobedience, and he had basically tested my willingness to respond to his need.

Proverbs 22:15 says: "Foolishness is bound in the heart of a child; but the rod of correction shall drive it far from him" (KJV).

In this verse the key word for me is *rod* and its place in the spanking process. Why does the Creator of our children tell us to use an object for spanking rather than our hand?

I believe it's because our Lord was warning parents about the ease with which children can be abused and beaten. My hand is too convenient. It is too easy to get into a habit of using this ever-ready implement to spank my child. One day, out of frustration, I might even find myself swinging around and slapping my child across the mouth. That would certainly not be a spanking.

Don't Take It Personally

Often, as parents, we take the things that our children do as personal affronts to our authority. Many parents, especially the pragmatic ones, like to sit the children down and give them a lecture on the things they are not to do. Once we have told them about the behaviors we will consider unacceptable, we actually expect them never to do those things again.

I remember when I was new at Sheridan House, telling a child why it was important not to go into the wood shop without an adult. I explained it to this little boy, and it all seemed very logical to me. When I felt confident that he understood, I left, knowing that he would never venture into that building unless escorted by an adult.

A few hours later, to my horror, I looked out a window and saw him playing in the wood shop. I was furious. It was not that he was in the wood shop that upset me as much as the fact that I took this as a personal issue. I had spent five minutes explaining to him why he shouldn't go in there, and then he had decided to disobey me. This little boy was taking me on! Or so I felt.

But in truth, it had very little to do with me. This child was not trying to do anything to challenge me. Nor was he choosing to disobey me. The wood shop was simply too inviting, and he wasn't convinced that there would be a consequence. This rebellious behavior was a time for responding with a spanking rather than frustration.

Select the Appropriate Paddle

When times of frustration come up and we are upset with the rebellious behavior of our children, we are prone toward overreaction. When that happens, looking for a paddle gives us time to cool off. However, parents should decide on an appropriate paddle that is not harmful or dangerous long before the situation arises that calls for its use. Failure to do this can also be detrimental.

I do not want my child to see my hand or any part of my body as the tool used for disciplinary purposes, but neither do I want to grab the first thing I see to use as a paddle. There are children who cower at the sight of a parent's raised hand. This conditioned response has become a reaction to slappings or beatings that came without warning from a parent. Few forms of child abuse are more devastating to the parent/child relationship. In situations such as these, the child has learned to respond to the parent's touch with fear, rather than warmth, acceptance, and love. Children should see a parent's hand as a tool of love. They should not be conditioned to be hand shy.

Let me say again: The hand is too convenient for overreaction on the part of the parent. In a perverse way, this reaction attempts to momentarily meet the needs of the parent's frustrations, and it is done in the guise of discipline.

In my little Superman's case, it meant that I needed to walk down the hall to the kitchen and get the wooden spoon. It was no longer funny at this point. I could hear him calling after me, "Please don't 'pank me, Daddy. I'm asleep." At that point I didn't know whether to laugh or cry.

What was the purpose of this exercise? If I wanted to meet my own needs, it certainly would have been easier to go back into his room and momentarily be his hero by announcing, "All right, Robey, I have decided to let you go this time. Next time, however, I will spank you." That response, though momentarily easier, would have been far from meeting the needs of my child. He had made the decision to push the "spank-me button," and it was my responsibility to love him enough to spank him.

Don't Spank in Anger

The spanking must be given in an instructive manner, not a vengeful fit of anger. As a parent, I must expect that my child will need to test my love and endurance as he grows up. Will I be able to respond to his need for boundaries without alienating our personal relationship?

As I walk down the hall for the wooden spoon, I have an opportunity to quickly reevaluate who this spanking is for. The spanking is not a way for me to vent my anger. It is a means for me to love and correct my child. With that in mind, it must be done in a calm, objective manner. There is nothing more frightening for a child than facing an out-of-control parent who is three to four times his size. Behavior that is out of control is not instructive; it's abusive and terrifying.

In the situation with my little Superman, I returned to Robey's room as soon as possible so that I would not delay the spanking. When I walked into the room, I told him to roll over, and I spanked him once or twice on the bottom. At that point the negative part of this disciplinary consequence was finished.

A Moment of Love

The next step in the spanking process is very important—and very strongly debated. Many professionals in the child development field say that the child should be left alone at this point to have an opportunity to think about the behavior that caused him to be spanked.

I respect the other professionals who believe this; but I do not find their approach to be necessary. Children do need time to reflect about what has happened; but I don't believe this reflection should be done at the expense of the child's fears. The child will already fear that his behavior might have done something to alienate him from the parent. For that reason the spanking needs to be done immediately, and in my opinion, the relationship also needs to be quickly reestablished.

The parent and the withdrawal of the parent's love are never to be perceived as part of the consequence. I am not the consequence for his unacceptable behavior. I want to make that point very clear. I will spank my child for rebellious behavior but I will still love the child. And I cannot establish my love for him by withdrawing myself from him. The child's moment of reflection about the incident needs to take place after the child has been reassured that the relationship is still intact.

Once the spanking had taken place, it was my job to stay in Robey's room for a moment, no matter how late I was going to be for my dinner appointment. I had a more significant appointment with my child.

I sat down on the side of the bed with Robey and held him for a few minutes. He was still at the age when he held up his hands for me to comfort him even though I had just spanked him. We sat for a moment and then I said to him, "Do you know why Daddy had to spank you?"

"Yes, Daddy," was his response.

"Why, Honey?" I asked.

"Because I got out of bed."

"That's right Robey," I said while I was holding him. "Please don't make me do that again. I hate spanking you; but I do love you, and when you disobey, I have to spank you. Please don't make Daddy have to spank you."

We spent some time together on his bed, and then I left and went out the door to the dinner. I also asked the baby-sitter to check on him in a little while.

I wanted to make sure Robey knew that I loved him regardless of his rebellious behavior and that I loved him enough to teach him to obey. That might mean being late for appointments from time to time and spanking him when I'd prefer to ignore or laugh at his behavior. As I see it, we have no option but to love our children enough to do the difficult things. Rebellion must be dealt with when they are young so that they will be teachable when they are older.

Summary

1. God's Word tells us that if we love our children, we will use the rod of discipline when they misbehave.

2. A parent's hand is too convenient to use as an instrument for punishment; it's too easily used in an abusive way. However, a paddle such as a wooden spoon is something that takes a moment to fetch, allowing a parent time to collect her- or himself and put things in their proper prospective. While getting the paddle, a parent can remind himself that the spanking is not to be administered to meet the frustration needs of the parent, but rather the disciplinary needs of the child.

3. Using the hand as the implement of spanking might cause a child to become "hand shy." When a child sees a hand coming at him, he may not know whether it is for affection or for correction. The child should never fear his parent's hand.

4. The spanking should not in any way destroy the parent-child relationship. It should be a quick form of punishment for rebellious behavior that just as quickly allows the parent to hold or hug the child as soon as the spanking is over.

5. Spanking is the best consequence for rebellious behavior—not just because it works, but primarily because it is God's plan. However, parents need to plan for spanking so that it can be done in a calm, instructive manner rather than a wild, frightening manner that terrifies the child.

13

Questions Often Asked about Spanking

PART OF THE SHERIDAN HOUSE ministry to the family is to present marriage and parenting seminars. At regular intervals during these seminars we have found it helpful to offer the participants opportunities to ask questions.

An interesting thing almost always takes place during these question times. Regardless of the topic being discussed, the questions inevitably turn to the subject of discipline. The topic discussed might have been sex education in the home, and yet most of the questions the parents will ask will pertain to spanking, boundaries, or some other disciplinary subject.

One of the limitations about book writing is that there is no opportunity to respond to the reader's questions. However, since the topic of spanking is such a crucial subject, I will attempt to anticipate some of the questions you might have by addressing some of those that are often asked at our seminars.

"You said that it is important to spank the child as soon as possible. What if I am furious at the time? Should I go ahead and spank him anyway so as to be prompt about it?"

It is important to spank the child as soon as possible. It is also important to deal with the child in a controlled manner, however. A child who sees his parent as wild and furious will be frightened of the parent he loves. The parent also stands a chance of overreacting when he or she deals with the child in a furious manner.

It is more important to be personally in control of one's self than it is to be prompt. There may be times when a parent has to say to his or her child, "Honey, go wait in your room. I will be in there in a little while. Right now I need to sit down."

That is the time a parent can collect himself and concentrate on the purpose of this consequence of wrong behavior: It is to correct and teach the child. It is not to vent parental anger.

"What happens when my child refuses to let me spank him?"
Parents must always be aware of what they can and cannot do. Only attempt to do the things that you are sure you're capable of doing. You can force a child to take a spanking, but that is not the optimum situation. The underlying purpose of spanking is to place a rebellious child back under a parent's authority. Physically forcing the child to submit to a spanking usually only proves that one person is bigger than the other.

Johnny's mom is trying to spank him and he faces her and says,. "No, I won't turn around." Johnny's mom has the option of forcibly turning him around herself or saying, "You are going to stay in this room until you are willing to turn around and be spanked." She might also tell him that he will not be permitted to do something he usually enjoys until he is willing to obey her and turn around.

Ideally Johnny's mom will stay in the room with him until this is done. The child needs to be taught that this kind of defiance is a serious matter and that his parent will not accept it.

No child is going to want to be spanked. It is only natural to try and find a way to avoid this unpleasant situation. A parent who is willing to take the time to allow the child to decide, on his own, to relinquish his will and accept the consequence will be helping the child learn a valuable lesson about respect for authority. So it is not only the actual spanking that teaches a lesson, but it is also the processes of relinquishing the will that teaches.

Parents should have a plan of action that requires the child to decide on his own to humble himself to the parents' authority. This kind of plan will help the child accept the mending of the relationship much better. It will allow the child to feel forgiven. If a parent attempts to wrestle the child to the ground, the mending of the relationship will be much more difficult.

There are no easy answers to this question. As with most important parental tasks, it takes a commitment of time.

"When I hit my child and he hit me back, it made me think that spanking only teaches my child to hit."
The very way this question is worded states a lack of understanding about the concept of spanking. *Spanking* and *hitting* have two different meanings. The word *hitting* pictures a frustrated parent who angrily

reaches around and backhands or slaps a child. In that picture there is no plan, nor is there a warning that says to the child, "What you are doing is a spankable offense. If you continue to do this, you are asking me to spank you."

A child who is dealt with by a parent who hits him in an erratic, unpredictable manner is certainly going to learn that hitting is the behavior to respond with when you are angry. He has no way of relating to hitting as unacceptable behavior because there hasn't been a consistent plan to teach it as unacceptable. He has seen his parent hit when angry. So in the child's world, this emotion and this behavior go hand in hand. It's only natural, then, that when he, too, is angry his impulse is going to be to hit back.

When spanking is handled in a calm manner and is part of an easy-to-understand parenting plan, the child will not associate spanking with anger. Also, spanking done with a paddle instead of the hand will not teach him to hit. It is very important to note, however, that this does not mean that the child will never respond to the parent by hitting.

Hitting might still be his natural response when the child is not getting his way. When another child takes his toy, he might respond by hitting or biting that child. The taking of the toy did not teach the child to hit. Rather, the cause was his own inability to deal with his anger.

A child will certainly be upset about being spanked. To vent his anger he might attempt to hit or bite the parent. He must be told that that behavior is also unacceptable; and if he does it again, he must be spanked again.

"At what age is spanking an appropriate consequence for rebellious behavior?"

The mother of John and Charles Wesley (she was also the mother of fifteen other children) said that each of her children knew about the wooden spoon by the time they were twelve months old. I don't know of any way to establish a hard-and-fast rule on appropriate ages for beginning to discipline children by spanking, because all children develop at different rates.

The time to begin spanking is when the parent is aware of the fact that the toddler understands the concept of *no*. That usually begins with a firm slap on the hand for touching things he has been told not to touch. The young child will begin to associate the parent's "No" with a decision.

The toddler will also associate the hand that is being slapped as the part of his body that has touched the item that is not supposed to be touched. In this instance and for this young a child, the slapping of the hand will be more effective than a wooden spoon on the bottom. The instant association is easier for the child to understand. He must decide to refrain from touching what he wants to touch, or his little hand will be slapped. Once that lesson has been taught, it is time to move on to spanking with something like a wooden spoon.

Is a child ever too old to be spanked? There is most assuredly a time in a child's life when spanking is no longer an effective consequence. In fact, most adolescents probably would rather be spanked than denied privileges. It's hard to say just when that magic age happens. Parents must decide with each child when that time to link responsibility to privilege has arrived. Once that decision is made, the next step is to determine what the young person will be denied if his behavior is not responsible and then tell him. Once again, he will be placed in the decision-making position.

Parents have said to me that their young person has pleaded, "Dad, couldn't we just go back to spanking? I'd much rather be spanked than have to stay in next Friday evening."

Each team of parents must decide when it's time to stop spanking. If the concept of spanking has been in place since early years, chances are good that the child has not needed to be spanked in several years anyway.

"You say that it is important to hold my child after he has been spanked. I know that it is important to hold him and let him know that I forgive him, but what if he does not want to be held?"

Some children want to be held after a spanking and some children do not. Just as adults vary as far as personal space and touching is concerned, so do children. That is their right and parents must respect it. If a child really does not want to be touched or hugged after a spanking, a parent can still make contact with the child by being close to him.

Some children would rather have a parent sit on the edge of the bed and simply be there for a while. It is important for the child to feel forgiven and loved even though he has had to be spanked. That can be communicated if the parent just remains in the room.

Other children, however, may act like they don't want to be touched, when in reality they do. When my daughter was nine years old, she would try to hide herself or isolate herself after being spanked. Torrey would lie on her bed, facing the wall, with her back to me. She initially gave me the impression that a hug was the last thing she wanted. Responding to what I thought was her desire not to be touched, I just sat on the bed near her.

One day, as I left her room after a spanking, I noticed Torrey rolling over to see if I was leaving. As I peeked back over my shoulder, I watched her tear-streaked face make an attempt at a smile. I had misjudged her body language. She wanted to make contact, but she wanted to make me work for it.

In her attempt to save face because she was humbled by the spanking, she wanted me to have to make an extra effort to hug her. In other words, she was asking, "How much do you love me, Daddy? Enough to make an extra effort to hug me when I appear unhuggable?"

The next time I was forced by her behavior to spank her, I stretched out next to her on the bed and gave her a few moments to calm down. Then I rolled over and gently squashed her against the wall until she started laughing. At that point I announced that I would squash her until she let me hug her.

That is most certainly not the approach to use with all children. Many children do need time to be by themselves, and would not respond well to being "squashed" by a loving daddy. Parents must be willing to take the time to assess their children to decide what they need. No two children are the same; but they all have a need to be loved, forgiven, and accepted.

"Don't you think that spanking is barbaric? It went out with the dark ages."

There will always be those who challenge the concept of spanking. I could show them that the process of spanking works because the punishment is instantly over and the parent-child relationship can quickly get back on track. I could also tell them that it deals with the basic problem being exhibited by the child, that of rebellion.

There are many reasons that spanking is the best option and I could strongly argue my opinion in its defense. It is not my opinion that is being attacked, however. Parents and many others in our society need to understand that they are not arguing with people's opinions about appropriate punishment, but rather with God's.

When our son, Robey, got an ear infection, we took him to the doctor. The physician prescribed medicine that he hated. We could have said that since he hated the taste of the medicine we wouldn't bother making him take it. Is it surprising that we never did that? Instead, we trusted the doctor's directions. Isn't it amazing how many people will trust mere humans and yet doubt the wisdom of God?

I am always quick to tell doubters that I will be more than happy to discuss the concept of spanking with them. From the start, however, I want them to know that spanking is not a theory, it is a directive from the Creator. They are not doubting my wisdom but His.

"What about the issue of child abuse?"

There are many children who suffer under the tyranny of beatings, whippings, slappings, and other forms of physical abuse. These are very different from spanking. The very purpose is completely opposite. Spanking is a controlled form of discipline in which a calm parent uses a wooden spoon or some similar paddle on the bottom of the child for the expressed purpose of correction. The child knows ahead of time that the behavior he is choosing to do carries with it the consequence of a spanking. The child also knows that this consequence is not done because the parent is mad or withdrawing love. Spanking done properly is followed by a time set aside with the expressed purpose of realigning the parent-child relationship. Spanking is used only for rebellious behavior.

Other forms of physical punishment may be done under the guise of being for the child's own good, but in reality they are forms of child abuse. Child abuse, in many forms, has risen to very serious proportions in our society today. We need to get serious about dealing with it by getting help for those families and children. Perhaps it is unfortunate that there is no required training for parents. After all, a person must get a license to drive a car so hopefully he won't drive it abusively, and yet anyone can have children. There is no doubt, physical child abuse must be dealt with.

Unfortunately, child abuse in the home has become such a serious problem that many parents have thrown out spanking altogether. This is like refusing to breathe because there are places where the air is polluted. You will do more harm to your child by not disciplining him for rebellious behavior than by spanking him.

Parenting with a plan means that we have an overall strategy to help our children grow up to be responsible adults. A small part of this plan requires that parents deal with rebellious behavior. The way to do that is to utilize God's directive to spank. That means to spank for the good and the love and the redirecting of the child, not to vent the frustration and anger of a parent who finds a child's behavior irritating. It is abusive to the future success of the child to raise him in such a manner that he does not know how to respond to leadership. Few things are more useless than a rebellious adult. But that's the kind of adult that may result from a parenting plan that does not include spanking.

Summary

1. It is important to spank a child as soon after the rebellious behavior as the parent is able to do it in a calm, mature, loving manner.

2. No child will want to be spanked. With a calm yet firm approach, the parent will need to help the child understand who's in charge.

3. Spanking is not "hitting" a child. It is a controlled, loving response that a child has asked for by his rebellious behavior.

4. A key time is after the spanking takes place. Make loving contact with the child. Re-establish the warm relationship. Attempt to hug the child.

5. Child abuse is a parental response that is out of control or demented. It is not a calm spanking to correct rebellious behavior. It's a wild response to meet a parent's needs rather than the child's needs.

PART IV

School: The Child's New Frontier

14

Preschool Day Care and Its Impact on Discipline

MY WIFE, ROSEMARY, spent the first eight years of our marriage as a public school teacher. One year she asked me into the classroom, for a day, to observe a few of her students. The children we were observing were overactive and finding it difficult to live within the boundaries of the class setting. She had been having a difficult time getting them to respond to her structure, so we thought we would look at these first-graders together.

Rosemary decided not to tell me which children I was to observe. It was my job to see if I could pick out the five children in question. I observed the class from the moment they arrived, until lunch; but within the first hour I could tell who they were.

After lunch I went into the teachers' lounge for a cup of coffee. While I was sitting in that moment of solitude drinking the coffee, an older teacher walked in. This lady had taught for years and had been a big encouragement to Rosemary in her early years. She asked me what I was doing that day in Rosemary's class, so we talked about the children for a while. The last statement this seasoned veteran made before we both left the lounge was, "I'll bet they grew up at a day-care center."

What an interesting thought. It was something that I could not test at the moment, but Rosemary decided to look into this theory at a later date, during parent conferences. Weeks later after a day of parent meetings, she came flying in the door. The first thing out of my wife's mouth was, "Bertha was right." Rosemary went on to remind me of my conversation with the older school teacher about the children who were having a difficult time responding to the classroom structure. It turned out that every one of the children Rosemary was having problems with had spent their preschool years in day care rather than in the home.

To be sure, there were other children in her classroom who had spent their preschool years in day care, and they were doing fine. It was interesting, however, that all of the students who were finding it difficult to keep their behavior within boundaries had spent a considerable part of their early years out of the home. How could this make such a difference?

So far I have been unable to locate any studies that reject or verify the hypothesis that children who spend their preschool years outside the home have more difficulty responding to the classroom structure. But there is much opportunity for conjecture.

Changing Boundaries

Consider three-year-old Bonnie. She wakes up in the morning as Mom and Dad are preparing to rush off to work. Everyone has his or her own agenda and responsibilities in Bonnie's home. After breakfast Bonnie is taken to a local day-care center and turned over to one of the workers. This particular child-care facility has twelve preschoolers per worker. The role of the child-care worker is primarily one of management. Her job description is to see to it that no one gets hurt or hurts others while moving on through the activities and exercises of the day.

The worker has her own personal set of boundaries as far as what is acceptable behavior and what is not. Due to the enormity of the assignment of keeping an eye on so many children, she has had to bend those personal boundaries considerably. After several hours, a new worker comes into the room and sets *her* behavioral boundaries for the next period of time. This new adult tolerates different behaviors than the previous adult. Little Bonnie learns that rules are not really cast in concrete. In other words, what she learns is that life depends on who's in the room.

Bonnie also learns that there are too many children for the adult in charge to deal with. It's not really quality of behavior that counts, but rather how not to get caught taking a toy away from another child. Survival of the fittest and deception are at a premium. Lessons of survival will certainly have to be learned by every child at some point in time, but preschool is too early an age for this. From age twelve months to age five or six is the prime time to establish a proper understanding of boundaries. These are the years when consistent boundaries are mandatory so that the child begins to grasp the need to respond to rules and discipline, rather than to the inconsistency of a system that keeps changing the players.

Bonnie's mom or dad picks her up after they have had a hard day at the office. Parent and child return home to what needs to be a sanctuary for each family member. Bonnie is excited to see her parents. Her parents are excited to be home away from the rat race; but now the housework and dinner responsibilities begin. Bonnie does not seem to be able to get the attention of her parents because they are so busy with other things around the house. To get their undivided attention, she whines or performs some other negative behavior. To keep Bonnie occupied, her parents give her a snack and turn on a children's evening television show. This is all under the guise of, "it's good for her because it's educational television." These parents have subcontracted their parental responsibilities to day care and TV. We cannot hire out our parental responsibilities or use something like television as a substitute. There are no "parenting experts" who will do a better or equally as good a job as a loving parent. Somehow many parents in our culture have been led to believe that subcontracting the job of parenting is possible, but it's not. No one can possibly enrich and emotionally enhance the development of a young child like his own healthy family.

Bonnie's behavior is affected by this lifestyle that is devoid of the time and attention of her parents. She quickly learns that life is a game of every one for himself, and her attitude is reflected behaviorally as she enters the primary grades.

Enhancing Burnout

There is another problem that Bonnie may face when she enters the primary grades in school. Kindergarten and the early grades are supposed to be fun. The motivational element to get these young children to be willing to learn new intellectual concepts is the fact that it's all new and exciting. This new institutional setting called "elementary school" counts on the fact that the children will be motivated by the newness of it all.

An institutional setting will not be new and exciting for Bonnie. She will have been in an institution for several years by the time she gets to first grade. In fact many professionals believe that she will stand a very good chance of facing "educational burnout." The children around her may be excited to learn because the experience is new to them. Bonnie, on the other hand, may be bored to tears. This boredom may contribute to her attitude and disruptive behavior in the school. Once again the preschool environment can have a negative impact on the future academic development of the child.

There are certainly those families that must have two incomes. There are also homes with single parents who must fulfill the role of provider as well as parent. For these families some form of day care for their children is a must. Perhaps when this situation exists in a family, however, some parameters could be followed that recognize the teaching of a proper response to boundaries as a very important step in the development of the young child. These lessons must also be coupled with a good, loving adult-child relationship. I believe that this area of early childhood development is much more significant than early academic development.

If day care is necessary, select a day-care situation that emphasizes relationships. This aspect can be analyzed by looking at the adult-child ratio. Equally as important is the amount of time that your child spends with the same primary-care worker. And the parent will want to interview that worker. Does this very significant adult have the same philosophy of life that you have as a parent? Is this adult's philosophy of life significant, you might ask? It is frightening to realize that the day-care worker will be spending more hours awake with your child than you will. That worker will be the one planting many ideas into that little "blank computer." Actually, I would even want to know about the grammar that the worker uses.

A more acceptable child-care situation would be for a relative or friend to care for the child during the day. At least a parent would have the opportunity of knowing the person who is helping to raise the child. Also, this home environment, with only a few other children, would more than likely be a place where the care giver could be more consistent in setting boundaries.

At the risk of passing on guilt to those who must use child care, I am compelled to close with this final statement. I have been in adolescent residential care since 1974. Because of my experience with the thousands of teen-agers who have lived in our residential settings here at Sheridan House, I know that day care at an early age has a negative impact on many children. And it is my opinion that child-care services stand a good chance of enhancing academic burnout. They can also play a part in causing a disruption in the development of the child's understanding of boundaries and responsibility. There is a price to pay when a parent goes off to work and places a young child in day care. That price is much more expensive than the weekly day-care fees. Parents must analyze whether day-care services are mandatory or just a matter of convenience. The cost as far as the child's growth is concerned is not cheap.

Summary

If child care is mandatory (and that is the first question that each family must address), take steps to see that the most beneficial arrangement is found. Ask the following questions:

1. What is the staff-child ratio?

2. How long will the same adult (primary-care worker) be with my child each day? In other words, will my child be forced to develop a relationship with several workers, or will he be able to work with the same one all the time?

3. What is the philosophy of life of that worker? Just because someone works at a Christian child-care center does not mean that he or she believes the same things you do.

4. Are there relatives or friends available who would want to take care of your child in their home?

15

The First Test of Freedom

CHILDREN HAVE MANY opportunities to test their self-control as well as their abilities to resist temptation. Every time they are away from parental control, they must decide whether they are going to continue behaving the way they have been taught or strike out on a new course.

School is usually the first consistent environment in which the child must learn to deal with self-control while away from parental authority. This is an important time for parent and child—and also a very frustrating time. It is not my objective here to discuss the virtues of one kind of school versus another. The purpose of this section is to write about the school environment facing most families today.

Children go off to school at varying ages. Unfortunately some go at such young ages that they are not yet prepared to make many of the decisions they will be challenged by peers to make. As prepared as a parent might want to make the child, this new world of decisions can be very frustrating.

This is the testing time, the time for a child to take into society what he has learned at home. The parent's role should continue to be pre-eminent. Mom and Dad must be in constant contact with the teacher to check on the child's progress, or visit the school in person.

Letting Go

"I don't know what happens to him when he gets to school. Tommy is such a good boy when he is at home, but when he gets into that playground at recess he goes wild. For a long time I didn't believe what his teachers were telling me. They must have my child confused with someone else, I thought. That was until I drove up and watched Tommy one day from my car. He was the roughest child out there."

This parent came to ask what she could do to get better control over her child when he was not around her. But the more significant question to start with was what she was doing with her child when he *was* around her. This particular parent was overly severe and controlling while Tommy was home. She made all his decisions for him. There were very few friends he was permitted to play with because she considered them all too unruly. And his solitary activities were limited, too. Climbing trees in the back yard, for example, was just too dangerous an activity for Tommy to be doing as far as she was concerned.

Tommy grew up under this very tight control. Mom made all his decisions, and she was always there to tell him what to do. Not so on the playground, however. Now this little boy was under a new system. There was no way for him to transfer the method he had learned at home to this new environment. At home his mother made all his decisions before he even had the opportunity to think about them.

School was different. On the playground, there was only one "parent" for two dozen children. The teacher couldn't anticipate all the decisions that needed to be made and prohibit activities that had not yet begun. Teachers must count on the fact that children are brought to school with some amount of personal discipline. To acquire this self-discipline, they must have been given the opportunity to make some of their own decisions at home in order to handle the many decisions that will be thrust upon them in this new environment.

Tommy's mother wanted to drop everything at 11:00 A.M. each day and help monitor the playground during recess. After all, it was quite apparent to her that they needed help. Perhaps one parent per child would be better, she thought. Deep down inside she wondered if recess was even necessary. Maybe Tommy would be better off if he were given something else to do during the play time.

What this mother really needed to do was let go. She needed to get out of the decision-making mode and set up a plan. Tommy needed to be given the opportunity to make decisions for himself. His mom could no longer use him as a little robot she was directing along the pathways of life. It might work for a while, but eventually he will outdistance her imaginary remote-control devices. She needed a parenting plan, rather than an overbearing voice.

Finally Tommy's mom came to the realization that she was either going to have to let him go—or plan on attending the senior prom with him a few years down the road. She was going to have to make some crucial decisions.

First of all, she had to see that her attempts to control him were detrimental to his growth. She had to learn to parent rather than control. "It seems like I am turning him over to the wolves, like I'm just letting him do poorly in school!" she protested. No, she wasn't letting him fail. She was letting him learn while she was still around to guide him. We might be able to control children while they are in our care, but we can never control their decisions when they are out of our sight. She had to let go and let him learn how to make good decisions for himself.

Second, this mom had to decide to trust the institution she was entrusting her child to. This institution, the school, was to be an extension of her parenting. Tommy's mom would have to trust its teachers and administrators to continue that work. But she also must understand that no person, teacher, or institution will make the exact same decisions for her child as she would.

I remember the battle that my wife and I went through when we wrote our wills. We were trying to decide who would rear our children if we were both killed. All of a sudden we found something wrong with the parenting skills of all our family and friends. We had to come to the conclusion that nobody was going to meet the grade, because we were so biased toward our own abilities when it came to this significant task. We simply had to trust—not just in the abilities of our friends, but rather in God.

I wonder what the mother of Moses went through when she had to turn her very young son over to a "pagan day-care center" at Pharaoh's palace. She did it out of faith—not faith in Pharaoh's palace, but faith in the knowledge that God loved her child even more than she did.

Once we have done our best to assure that our children are in the best educational environment we can locate and afford, that same trust must come into play. Certainly there will be times of doubts. There will also be times when a parent questions school decisions that are made. The bottom line on this trust is very important, however.

When the school reports that the child has done something that is an unacceptable behavior, don't battle with the institution that is supposed to be your extension. If there are legitimate doubts about the validity of the school's report, question it in private. Set up a meeting with the teacher, but back her up in front of your child. The minute your child sees a lack of confidence between parent and teacher, the child may do everything in his power to further that division with statements such as,

"She always picks on me, Mom. No one else has to do these extra assignments." Work hard to maintain a solid parent-teacher relationship.

Third, Tommy's mom had to set up a plan that would allow the teacher to communicate with her. This mother needed to know how Tommy was doing on a daily basis. She also needed to decide how she was going to deal with positive and negative behaviors. This was a new approach for her. Now she would be dealing with behavior after the fact, rather than trying to run out in front and stop the behavior before it had taken place. Now the child would be forced to make decisions.

The Daily Behavior Report

A daily written report from the teacher would be an excellent way to help parent-teacher communication. The simplest way for the teacher to squeeze this into her daily schedule would be for the parent to create an easy-to-use form that pertains specifically to the child's behavior. Like the one shown in the following example, the form should also be set up in such a way as to allow the teacher to communicate the child's progress or needs to the parent in a matter of a minute.

BEHAVIOR REPORT

Date _____   Teacher _____

Behavior	Excellent	Fair	Poor
Keeping hands to self	___	___	___
Not climbing fence	___	___	___
Talking nicely to other children	___	___	___
Showing respect to teachers	___	___	___
Only needing to be told once	___	___	___
Playing fair	___	___	___

The form should be as specific as possible in describing the personal behavior of the child. The form should be discussed with the teacher to get his or her input about behaviors to be mentioned. The important thing is that parent and teacher are together on what each item describes.

The most important step in using this form comes next. The form must be explained to the child so that he or she understands what each item refers to. "Tommy, explain to me what it means to play fair. What are some examples of when children don't play fair?"

As the child brings home the report each day, it needs to be handled as a significant matter in his life. It should not be something that is set on the dining-room table to be looked at when the parent has time. The parent must promptly take time to look at each day's report.

Parents will also need to decide what it will mean to the child when he receives a "poor" on his report. It may mean going to bed fifteen minutes early or writing his spelling words five times each. It should be something that will be established as a consistent consequence.

Parents must also decide how to handle his progress. What will happen when Tommy comes home with a report that says he was excellent? Much of the time parents are just hunting for deficiencies and ignore behavior when it is acceptable or good. The child must know that the parents are excited about his efforts to be good.

A reward that is used around the Barnes household is one that can justifiably be debated. There are many who say the use of food as a reward is establishing bad habits for the future. Perhaps there are some adults who have grown up where desserts have been used to reward certain behavior, and as adults they have continued to reward themselves on into obesity. That could be true. After all, it's back to an understanding of personal discipline, isn't it?

When the children were young in our house and they did something well, we went out for ice cream. "Look at this paper of Torrey's! It's fantastic! I guess that means it's time for ice cream," we would exclaim. Developing some sort of positive response to the child's improved behavior is extremely significant. If there is a way to do it and brag about it to the world at the same time (we would always tell the person behind the ice cream counter what we were celebrating), it is sure to have a more lasting effect.

On the other hand, a decision will also need to be made about what to do when Tommy loses his report or "forgets it." There should be a logical consequence that has already been established so that the parent and the system don't fall apart just because the paper is lost. This consequence—perhaps going to bed early—should not be overly severe; but it should make the point that the parent wants the report brought home.

Some parents may want to have at their fingertips the home phone number of the teacher for those days when the report is not completed perhaps because there was a substitute, or because the teacher forgot. Children are not likely to lose things that are important to them (my children never lost a cookie). The report can become a significant part of their routine, especially if it helps them get positive feedback from the parent.

The time will soon come when Tommy only needs to bring home the report from school once a week. As he continues to progress, the report can eventually be eliminated totally. The positive feedback from the parent can never be eliminated, however, or it won't be long until the child will need, and possibly want, his daily report again.

The parent then needs to get out of the way of her child's learning and love him. Part of teaching the lesson of discipline is allowing the child the privilege of making decisions. This parenting process is one of letting go. The child will need the opportunity to practice more and more freedom as time goes on. This freedom begins when the child starts to walk. His freedom is never so evident as when he goes out the door to school. This is only the beginning of trusting in your parenting plan and trusting in God for the growth of your child.

Summary

1. School is the first extended period of time for which most parents must let go. It is a time for allowing the child to practice the personal disciplinary skills he has learned at home. A parent who continues to try to be right there, controlling all the decisions the child must make, will hurt the child's growth. He will not be given the opportunity to learn how to make decisions and accept their outcome.

2. As parents, we must learn to accept the institutions that we are turning our children over to. Once we have decided that this is the best educational opportunity available for the child (from a financial point of view as well as geographical), then we must move forward with a positive attitude. Learn about the school, and learn to trust it.

3. Parents can help their child, if he is having disciplinary problems in school, by establishing a quick and easy way of daily communication with the teacher. With the help of the school or teacher, create a form that will assist this communication.

4. Establish a plan to use this form to give your child feedback about his behavior.

5. Describe the form to the child and make sure he understands it.

6. Let go of the child so that he can learn to make his own decisions.

7. Reward positive progress, and have a consequence for negative responses.

16

School and the Older Child

"IT SEEMS THAT the minute my child went off to middle school, we lost him. At that point he became very disenchanted with his home and his family." This was the comment of a frustrated parent.

Many things take place simultaneously when a child reaches middle-school age. The child enters puberty and is not quite sure what is happening to his body. To make matters worse, many parents don't tell their children about this sudden activation of hormones. The child is going through dramatic physiological changes, to say nothing of the emotional changes, yet too often parent and child don't discuss these happenings. There is an obvious silence on this topic.

As a result, the child is left without information about the changes taking place within his mind and body. Some parents act as if teen-agers are having significant discussions about these matters with their peers. It may surprise Mom and Dad to know that their son is not walking down the halls at school saying to his friends, "How's your puberty going today?" Many young people are simply left uninformed.

This is the beginning of the breakdown of communication between parent and child. "My parents used to talk to me, but now they seem almost afraid of me," an adolescent might say. Realizing that this could be perceived by some as a difficult topic for parent and child to discuss, outside resource materials should be used. One of the best is the audio-tape series "Preparing for Adolescence" by Dr. James Dobson. This set of tapes is most effective when listened to by parent and child together. Listen to a tape for a few minutes and allow the teen-ager to turn it off at strategic times for discussion. If the teen-ager is too inhibited to ever turn the recorder off, then the parent must do it. The tapes should be used as a discussion stimulator.

A friend of mine listened to these tapes with his twelve-year-old daughter while driving in the car. He told me that her face was screwed up in a look of disapproval while they drove and listened. She was doing everything in her power to appear disinterested. But at the end of side one he reached out to turn it over, only to find that his daughter had beaten him to it. Quick as a flash, she had flipped it over and popped it back in. Of course, then she resumed her posture of looking disinterested.

It doesn't matter how secure a teen-ager may look, he still needs and wants a relationship with his parents. The relationship is different at this point, however. Parents need to allow their child more space than when they were small children. The young person needs the freedom to make more decisions about his life. Mothers and fathers are often very frustrated during this stage of parenting. "I feel like my teen-ager doesn't want to be within a mile of me," parents of teen-agers have been heard to say. Though they may need more space to practice decision making and evaluate the values their family has raised them with, they are still desperate for a parent-child relationship.

The teen-ager even goes so far as to play a game of "figure me out" when you invite him to go places with you or the family. You might say, "Billy, we're going to the park this Saturday for a family picnic." Most likely Billy's first words of response will be, "Do I have to go?"

The parent feels that Billy doesn't want to go and so he shouldn't have to go. On the surface, the teen-ager feels like he would rather stay home. Deep down inside, his feelings of alienation have caused him to further isolate himself, even from the family that loves him. Teen-agers should be permitted the opportunity to be excused from some, but not all, family activities. They must be reminded that family activities are still important enough for their participation. Even when teen-agers seem alienated, they still want to feel needed and loved by the family. Teen-agers also need to feel as if they are part of something good rather than separate isolated units.

Adolescent Alienation

The middle-school setting plays a very significant part in the teen-ager's feeling of alienation. Prior to this point in the education of the child, he or she had the opportunity to develop a relationship with a surrogate parent. The teacher he spent the whole day with was a person that he got to know well. For many young people the elementary school teacher was someone with whom he could share personal problems.

At the time when the teen-ager enters puberty, and his parental relationships might have become strained, the middle-school setting sometimes throws him a curve. There is no longer such an easy opportunity to establish a strong student-teacher relationship. Instead of having the same teacher all day, the system changes in middle school. Due to the specialization of education, the child moves to a different teacher each hour. There is little time or opportunity to get to know the teacher in any way deeper than the purely academic relationship.

This can be a real loss to many children. During their early years, many have a very good relationship with the elementary-school teacher, and then, when they need positive adult input more than ever, it's not available. Now, when the parent-child relationship is strained the most, that teacher-child relationship is no longer built into the system.

I used to think that enemy spies had decided to take over America by sabotaging the middle schools of our land, pumping a negative gas into the air ducts of all the middle schools across our country. Why else would children who loved school during their elementary years all of a sudden become very negative about it upon entering middle school?

I finally realized that it was not a plot. It was just that too often the school system simply lets teen-agers down in middle school. At a time when they desperately need adults with whom they can communicate, this is no longer made easy by the system. If parents aren't quick to fill the gap, their teen-ager's new communication companion is either a peer or television.

This does not need to happen, however. Parents can maintain a relationship with their teen-ager if they are willing to give it the time that is necessary. This is the time to go on "dates" with the child and spend hours listening rather than minutes lecturing. A teen-ager who feels he is still important to his parents and worthy of their ear is less likely to rebel in significant ways.

When rebellion does occur, however, it usually takes place in the school setting first. The frustration for the parent lies in the fact that very little can be done to help the child work diligently at his education. The lectures about the future and questions such as "Don't you want to live in a nice house like this someday?" don't seem to yield the desired results. The teen-ager knows that he has an upper hand.

Fortunately all is not lost. The older child can be helped to do better in school. Many of these lessons could have been taught when the child was in elementary school. Some of the problems could have been made less critical in middle school. But the job of parenting never ends. If anything, it becomes more in-depth than ever as the child enters his teen-age years.

Stay in Touch

Parents of middle schoolers need to maintain a close relationship with their child's school, either directly with the teachers or through the guidance counselor. Most parents of children this age feel as if they are left with no options but to wait for the report card or interim reports. This does not need to be the case.

If the indications are that the child is rebelling by falling behind in school, the parent needs to immediately make contact with the guidance counselor and ask for help. The question to ask is, "What does the school have available to help my child work up to his abilities?"

Most schools can provide a progress report. This is a report that the child can take to each teacher, usually at the end of each week, to find out how he is progressing in school. For schools that don't have one of these reports available for the parent, a sample progress report has been provided at the end of this chapter.

The progress report should focus on behavior more than it focuses on grades. If the behavior is redirected, the grades will change. If the child gets to class on time with his homework done and he completes his class work, his grades will improve.

A progress report, checked off by all the child's teachers, can assess that behavior. What if, after two weeks, the child's behavior has not changed? At that point it may be time to once again meet with the guidance counselor. One of several conclusions can be reached. Is the work too hard for the child due to special areas of difficulty? Is the progress report not assessing the correct areas? More than likely the answer will be that the weekly report covers too long a time period.

There are many young people who will get back on track sooner if their behavior is assessed on a daily basis rather than a weekly basis. The same report can be used by the student and teachers each day.

It's important to know that this plan will not be very exciting to the child. Parents should listen to the child and yet be ready to place the responsibility for this action where it belongs. "I can't believe that you're making me do this, Mom. It's so embarrassing to take this up to the teacher's desk at the end of each class," he might say.

One parent responded with, "Billy, I'm not the one who has caused you to have to bring home a daily progress report. You have caused us to get to this point."

"How long will I have to do this, Mom?" Billy asked.

"If you can go for two weeks, bringing home a progress report every day that is signed by every teacher and that is a good report, then we will drop it back to just once a week. When you bring home three good weekly progress reports in a row, we will drop them altogether."

Billy was also told that if, after they stopped the reports, the guidance counselor told her that he had started to slide again, they would go back to getting weekly reports from each teacher.

"Mom, what happens if I forget to have a teacher fill out the report or I lose it?" Billy asked.

This very wise mother was ready for this challenge. "Billy," she began, "if I gave you a one-hundred-dollar bill, do you think you would lose it or forget to pick it up?"

"Not a chance, Mom" Billy answered.

"Well, then, I want you to treat this progress report like a one-hundred-dollar bill," his mother began to explain. "This progress report will be very significant to your afternoons and evenings. If you come home and have forgotten to have one of the six teachers fill out their portion of the form, then you will have to do a half-hour of extra work that afternoon or evening. If you lose the whole form, the dog eats it, or there is a hold up on the bus and it is stolen, then you will have to do a half-hour of work for each class on the form."

"But Mom!" Billy gasped, "I've got six classes. You're going to make me do three hours of work after dinner just because I don't bring the report home?"

"No, Billy," his mother quickly responded, "I'm not the one causing you to have to do the work. You will be the one. I don't want you to do any work after school or in the evening. I want you to have a nice time. But I love you enough to see to it that you do the work if you cause it to have to happen. You will cause it to happen if you don't bring the report home each afternoon."

Billy's mom went on to explain that it was his attitude toward school that got him to this point of having to take daily progress reports around. It was her love for him that would do everything possible to help him work up to his potential.

The first two days went very well. Humbling though it was, Billy took the report to every teacher each day. On the third day, however, Billy lost the sheet part way through the day. He assumed that one of the teachers forgot to give it back, and in the rush to get to his next class, Billy forgot it.

No matter how much he pleaded, he still got three hours of work after school. Never again did Billy lose that sheet. Once, part way through the day, he couldn't find it and quickly took out a piece of blank paper and created a new progress report. At the end of the day he caught up to his earlier teachers and asked them to sign it. He had become a believer in the plan.

Billy's mom also did an excellent job of encouraging the teachers to be helpful enough to take fifteen seconds at the end of class to fill out the report. After two or three days she wrote a note to each teacher and thanked them for taking the time to help her help Billy.

This positive note went a long way toward helping the teachers do this extra task. It helped so much that one of them called one evening (Billy's mom had put her phone number at the bottom of the note and encouraged them to call) to ask if the reports had been discontinued. This surprised her since the woman's initials had been on the bottom of all the reports.

As the conversation continued, it became apparent that Billy was testing the effectiveness of these reports by forging the teacher's signatures. For punishment Billy was assigned work for the reports that were forged. It was also now apparent that Billy's mom was going to have to pay more attention to the signatures on the reports, as well as check with the guidance counselor every now and then.

Finally Billy completed the necessary period of time to be able to reduce the reports to Fridays only. On that final daily report, Billy's mom notified the teachers of this fact with a note on the bottom. Eventually Billy was able to drop the reports altogether.

Billy learned several lessons. He found that it was his responsibility as to when he could stop taking the reports. It was a waste of time arguing with his mother since she always had the same response to his question: "I don't know when you will be able to go to school without these reports, Billy. You tell me; it's up to you."

Billy also found that his grades improved dramatically. He wasn't perfect after this one time with the reports. His parents found that he needed the reports again for a while to get on track during the next school year.

Disciplined Study Skills

Parents can go one extra step with those young people who are falling behind. They can help them develop the discipline of decent study skills.

It has been said that you can lead a horse to water, but you can't make it drink. Similarly, some parents become very frustrated that they can't seem to motivate their young people to study. One thing to remember is that you may not be able to make the horse drink, but you can certainly salt their oats!

Many middle-school students have no study skills whatsoever. To be able to attack the new concepts that they are being taught in secondary grades today seems an insurmountable task. It's almost impossible to do if they don't know how to study.

Parents can be of great assistance to their teen-agers if they help organize the students' study time. "Son, it appears to me that I have made a mistake as far as your studies are concerned," a father could begin. "You have fallen behind in your work and homework, and that may be because I haven't helped you discipline your study time wisely. From now on we will set aside time from seven to eight-thirty for you to sit at the dining-room table to study."

Granted, no one can make a child learn. We can, however, set a more conducive atmosphere. When a student has gotten to the point that he is handling his homework in a more responsible way, the parent can begin to let go.

"Johnny, you have been doing much better at completing your school work. If you would like, we could purchase you a desk so that you can do this work each evening at your own desk in your room."

Obviously, the next step is to allow the student to set his own homework time. "As long as you're able to do this well, you can be the one to decide when the work gets done. If, however, you begin to fall behind, we will have to go back to the old homework plan. I am very proud of how well you're doing."

The teen-age phase of life is a testing period. Parents must pick and choose their battles wisely. School battles may be an area worth fighting since they affect so much of a child's future. Parents must be willing to analyze the child's academic ability in a realistic manner. Every child will not be going to an Ivy League school, nor should every child go to college.

The key parenting goal is to help a child become self-disciplined in the area of academic development. That means to first analyze any problem areas: school behavior, poor grades, etc. Second, the parents must do what they can, in conjunction with the school, to set parameters that will help structure the child to have the best possible opportunity for improving. Once again the parent can only set parameters to help the child. The child may still go to sleep, refuse to work within that fence, or choose to jump the fence altogether. But when progress is seen, parents must be ready to relax the reins of control and give the child more freedom.

The ultimate goal, after all, is not good grades in school. The ultimate goal for this young person is to help him understand how to be self-disciplined enough that he will reach his full potential when he is an adult. Helping a middle-school student become self-disciplined to overcome obstacles will eventually help this emerging adult learn to overcome the bigger obstacles of life.

Summary

1. The child that is in middle school is expected to be at a point of development where he can be more self-disciplined. However, factors such as hormonal changes leading to mood swings, the change in the school configuration, and the changing parent-child relationship can make growth in self-discipline difficult.

2. Parents can assist the academic progress of the child by using a school progress report.

3. A progress report will be an objective tool in the parent-child discussions about school.

4. The progress report will place the responsibility for progress on the child's shoulders.

PROGRESS REPORT

FOR _____ DATE _____

1. CLASS: _____ Behavior   Respect for
                       (good/bad) _____   Authority _____
   TEACHER: _____   Classwork   Homework
                       Completed _____   Completed _____
                       Has Materials _____ Tardy _____

   Teacher's Comment: _____

   Teacher's Signature: _____

2. CLASS: _____ Behavior   Respect for
                       (good/bad) _____   Authority _____
   TEACHER: _____   Classwork   Homework
                       Completed _____   Completed _____
                       Has Materials _____ Tardy _____

   Teacher's Comment: _____

   Teacher's Signature: _____

3. CLASS: _____ Behavior   Respect for
                       (good/bad) _____   Authority _____
   TEACHER: _____   Classwork   Homework
                       Completed _____   Completed _____
                       Has Materials _____ Tardy _____

   Teacher's Comment: _____

   Teacher's Signature: _____

4. CLASS: _____ Behavior   Respect for
                       (good/bad) _____   Authority _____
   TEACHER: _____   Classwork   Homework
                       Completed _____   Completed _____
                       Has Materials _____ Tardy _____

   Teacher's Comment: _____

   Teacher's Signature: _____

5. CLASS: _____ Behavior   Respect for
                       (good/bad) _____   Authority _____
   TEACHER: _____   Classwork   Homework
                       Completed _____   Completed _____
                       Has Materials _____ Tardy _____

Teacher's Comment: _____

Teacher's Signature: _____

6. CLASS: _____ Behavior   Respect for
                     (good/bad) _____   Authority _____
   TEACHER: _____ Classwork   Homework
                     Completed _____   Completed _____
                     Has Materials _____   Tardy _____

Teacher's Comment: _____

Teacher's Signature: _____

Homework

1. CLASS _____

2. CLASS _____

3. CLASS _____

4. CLASS _____

5. CLASS _____

6. CLASS _____

Parent's Name: _____ Phone: _____

17

A Time for Structured Freedom

YEARS AGO I WATCHED a friend as he spent his last few years with his daughter before she went off to college. I remember one of the things he did that initially surprised me. When his daughter began her senior year of high school, my friend started a new plan where her curfew was concerned. He let her set her own time to be in. I can still remember how shocked I was when I heard about it. I wanted to say to him, "Jack, this is South Florida. I can't believe that you're going to let her come in at night whenever she wants to in a part of the world like this." I was amazed that he would give her so much freedom.

Later on that year he explained his parenting plan. "All along I have been training and structuring the lives of my children," my friend explained, "but now is the time that they must practice." He went on to talk about the fact that his daughter was just a few months away from being out on her own. When she went to college, she would be responsible for setting her own curfew without anyone looking over her shoulder. He wanted her to have the opportunity to practice for a while when she still lived at home.

"On a Friday evening she comes and tells me when she will be in and where she is going," he continued his explanation. "I confess that sometimes I am a little bit concerned, and often we discuss things such as the wisdom of going to a party where she doesn't know the hosts. The key to this arrangement is that she tells me what time she wants to come in and then she sticks to that time.

"Yes, I can see what you're thinking, Bob," he said. "It is sometimes later than I would like her to be out." This statement anticipated my question. "Next year she will be coming home each night to an empty dormitory room with no one to meet her or even care if she comes in. I want her to practice this area of personal discipline this year while I am here to love her when she makes mistakes," he said.

"What happens if she gives you a time that she will be in and she violates that time?" I asked.

"If my daughter does that without calling first," he answered, "then she knows there will be a consequence for her lack of consideration and irresponsibility."

As we talked, I could see that my friend had certainly not taken the easy way out. It would have been so much simpler to make statements like, "As long as you live in this house, this is the way we will always do it." Instead he had chosen to bend and let his daughter practice the independence that would be dumped on her in a matter of months.

Ready or Not . . .

High school is not an easy time for parents because, like it or not, it is a time that our society thrusts opportunities of independence on our children. These opportunities in our world are like the old game, "ready or not, here I come." Along with high school comes such experiences as dating and the sexual disciplines that are necessary to stay pure. High school also ushers in the driver's license and the discipline of controlling the lust for power that an automobile gives a person. There is also the more accelerated access to drugs and alcohol that the high-school student has.

All of these areas require discipline if the lusts are to be conquered. Unfortunately we are not talking about the personal discipline of the parent to know what to let the child do or not do. It is also irrelevant to discuss whether the parent is personally disciplined enough to stand his ground and keep the teen-ager from these temptations. We're talking about the personal discipline of the young person to learn to walk away from life's temptations.

I had the privilege of going to a Christian college. The period of time in my life that I arrived there was interesting. Not only was I not a Christian, but I had really not been to church much at all. At this particular college there were many students from missionary families as well as others who had grown up in pastors' homes. I remember how shocked I was my freshman year to find out that some of the girls with the loosest sexual morals were those from ministerial homes. They got to college and could not handle the freedom that they were given for the first time. Their parents had sheltered them so much that the freedom afforded them while away at college was just too much. Many of these students made some disastrous decisions that affected the rest of their lives. It wasn't the fault of the college. Rather, it was the fault of an overly restrictive parenting plan, one that had allowed no opportunity to practice freedom before these young people went out the door into total freedom. There was no easing them into the world.

A friend of mine kept his oldest daughter very close to home, rarely letting her go to events that were overnight activities. This young girl responded in a different way when she got to college. She didn't give in to the temptations. Instead, she begged to quit school and return home at Christmas time. It was too hard to be away making her own decisions.

I question whose needs are being met in these overly restrictive situations. Are the parents really trying to meet the training needs of the child, or are they trying to protect themselves from any problems until after the child is out the door? Many girls have even gotten married motivated primarily by what they perceived as an opportunity for freedom.

Structuring the Child's Freedom

High school is a finishing school. Every young person is different and thus can handle different amounts of freedom at various times in his development. The freedom that we are discussing here can best be referred to as a "structured freedom." This means that there are still boundaries. The young person knows that when he abuses his freedom (and he will), the opportunities will become more limited for a period of time. A parental plan of structured freedom opens up another very special door between parent and child. When the structure for a teenager remains very rigid, there is very little opportunity for parent-child discussion. When there is discussion, it is usually in the form of one-sided begging or arguing.

Structured freedom, on the other hand, offers the young person the opportunity to talk with the parent about his life. He knows that his parent is listening to what he is saying. It becomes very obvious that the parent is interested in what the young person is asking to do since he is being given this new freedom. Parent and teen-ager naturally grow in the area of communication. No longer is the typical parental answer a quick *no!* Now there are discussions. It also opens up an opportunity of trust and intimacy. The teen-ager can hear his dad say that he does not really agree with what the child is asking to do, but that he will bend and permit it.

The child learns many things here. He learns what the parent's opinion is without having to debate it. Parent and child are able to discuss without as much arguing. The child begins to learn how to deal with conflicting points of view in a mature manner. This child also sees that his dad is willing to trust him—maybe even forgive him, since he didn't do so well in this particular area a few weeks ago.

In many homes young people are used to hearing the word *no*. Now, as the parent is offering the teen-ager some opportunities of freedom, a new relationship begins to grow. Though the child will still hear some *no's* to his requests, he will at least be able to discuss them.

This can be the beginning of a great parent-child relationship because each participant sees that the other person is listening. Instead of closing out the child by trying to fit every decision into a nice, neat pigeonhole, the parent who uses a plan of structured freedom has an opportunity to get much closer to the child.

This parent will also have a much greater opportunity to say *no*. "Billy, I have been thinking about what you are asking me to do. You know that I have been trying to say yes to everything that I feel God would permit me to. Staying overnight at the beach on prom night is one of the few requests that you have come to me with that I cannot, in good conscience, say yes to. Your mother and I have decided to offer an alternative, if you want it. We will be happy to sponsor a big after-midnight-until-dawn party and breakfast here at the house. That's only if you want it. I am sorry, but it's the best I can do."

Rather than constantly hearing edicts from his dad, Billy will have learned to talk. The *no's* in life will be easier to take because there are some *yes's* to balance them.

These discussions will also give parent and child the opportunity to talk about some key issues that might never come up otherwise. The child now has an investment in the way he asks and explains himself. Parent and child will invariably have more significant talks about drugs and sex as they discuss reasons involved in the decision-making process. Structured freedom helps the young person have the chance to talk about situations he meets and has to face in life, and they can be discussed with more freedom.

This plan also gives the teen-ager an opportunity to practice making decisions. How many times have parents said that they wished their children made better decisions? Yet these are often the very parents who never let their children have the freedom to make any decisions on their own. With this freedom comes the opportunity and responsibility to make decisions.

Young people must have the opportunity to practice before they leave home, or the world will eat them alive. In boot camp there were war games, and they were serious business. There were many times when some people even got hurt. The games weren't done to hurt people. On the contrary, they were done to prepare soldiers for the real war. The recruits practiced the war-time situations so that they could look at their mistakes and be helped to correct them. If boot camp was all done in a classroom setting, with no actual practice, many more lives would be lost in a real, war-time battle.

High school is that last opportunity for the parent to begin to let go while still staying very close to the child to instruct him. Some think that high school is a time that requires less parenting. Actually, the opposite is true. It is a time of talking and growing closer, even as you are letting go. How much does a parent let go during high school? I was once asked, "Couldn't you print out a list of what to let go of?" Sorry, but that can't be done. Every young person is different. They can handle different responsibilities at different times of life. No two children mature at the same rate. And letting go is first predicated on the assumption that there was a disciplinary plan for the child when he was young.

Letting go is more than trusting in the child or in a parenting plan, however. It's really trusting in the fact that God loves my children more than I do. In fact, He sent His Son to die in their place. Letting go must be accompanied by prayer—prayer that God will help the parent make the right decisions as to where to let the young person practice freedoms and that God will help the parent overcome any failures.

Parents will all be forced to let go at some point. It makes more sense to let go when the teen-ager is spending his final seasons at home so that the family can be there to help.

Summary

Letting go is a process that must take place from birth on. Never is it more obvious than when the child is in high school, however. It necessitates a structured freedom.

1. Structured freedom means that the parent begins to let go and let the teen-ager make more and more personal decisions.

2. Structured freedom means that as the parent places more personal responsibilities on the teen-ager's shoulders, the lines of communication will naturally open. Both parent and child will want to talk as they discuss these decisions.

3. Structured freedom lets the child know that as long as he is able to handle making good decisions he will be permitted to continue to do so. It means that the parent will have to risk allowing the teen-ager to make some difficult decisions.

4. Structured freedom means that when the teen-ager makes poor decisions or doesn't live up to his agreements, the structure becomes tighter for a while.

5. Structured freedom allows practice and builds trust.

PART V

Discipline: Correction That Teaches

18

The Big Failures

THE SUMMER BEFORE my sophomore year of college I worked two jobs. The primary reason for the jobs was to purchase and pay off a car before I went back to school that fall. My previous year in college had not been spectacular academically. Somehow I had gotten by, however.

As the summer ended and I prepared to drive back to school in my own car, I could sense my dad's apprehension. He was worried that the car would cause my studies to drop off. The night before I left home he gave me a pep talk, and I'm sure that I hardly listened. He said, "Bob, be careful not to let this car interfere with your studies. This is a very important time in your life."

That first semester back at school I was working hard at being Mr. Man About Campus at Maryville College. Not only did I have a car, but I also decided to pledge one of the local fraternities.

I was doing everything but studying, and I could tell by my dad's weekly letters that he knew it. In fact it made me mad that he could sense it from five hundred miles away. His letters once again told me about the perils of flunking out of school. I can still see it typed on his stationery: "What you do in college will determine what you do in life."

Finally the school year ended, and I returned home to work for the summer. I wasn't home two weeks when a letter from the college arrived in the mail, announcing that the school no longer needed me. I had flunked out. Actually I was somewhat surprised. Could this really be happening to me? The very thing my dad had continually warned me about had come true.

Letter in hand, I stormed out the front door of our house. As I got to my car, a very familiar sound came from the house. "Bob," my dad shouted from the window of his study, "come on upstairs and talk to

116

me." I knew my dad had received a copy of the same letter I got. If I went back in the house, I was sure to hear "I told you so" for the next hour. And I was not in the mood to be lectured by my dad.

In our home, we had been taught respect for authority, and I had abided by that teaching all my life. All my life, that is, until I reached the age of sixteen. Everything caved in at that age. I had been very close to my mom, and when I was sixteen, she died of cancer. As is understandable, it was a very difficult time for all of us. For some reason I vented my anger over Mom's death at my father. These had been very difficult years for our relationship. More than anything I was tired of being the one who was always wrong.

I could have continued to get in my car that day instead of responding to his request to come upstairs and talk. It probably would not have surprised him much. Instead, I braced myself and walked back into the house. After all, he had been paying for most of my education. The least I could do, now that I had failed, was endure his lecture.

"What Are We Going to Do about This?"

When I got to his study upstairs, I found him sitting at his desk, waiting for me. He watched me enter without saying a word, then asked me to sit down. I will never forget his first words. "What are we going to do about this letter from school?" he asked.

"What do you mean?" I responded without looking up at him.

"Are we going to just accept it as the only option, or do you think that we could do something about it?" Dad continued.

"Dad, I don't know what else to do. They said that I'm through," I said, starting to get angry.

I wondered what he was getting at. Was he just trying to rub salt in the wound? It sure was a different approach. So far, no "I told you so" had been said.

Dad continued in a very calm manner. "I think that we need to get you the first available ticket back to Maryville. You could meet with the Dean of Academic Affairs tomorrow and find out what it would take to get back into school."

The next thing I knew we were calling the airlines that very day, then hopping into the car. As we walked through the airport together, he stopped me and said, "There's one more thing before you get on the plane."

Here it comes, I thought. *Here comes the lecture that has been brewing up inside of him for the past several hours.* Dad looked me right in the eye and said, "Here's some pocket money; call me tomorrow after you have met with the dean. Then we'll decide what to do next and what plane to book for your return flight."

I was in shock. It was my failure, and yet he kept using the word "we" as if he had played a part in it. Actually his approach started a big change in my life. Even though I deserved the lecture, he decided to jump on my team, or rather, jump on my sinking ship. He gave me the courage to return to school the next day and beg my way back in.

As it turned out, there were several of us who had received the same letter. I was the only one to immediately return to campus, however. Apparently, I was the only one whose father had decided to help a son "bail water." Consequently, I was the only one who got back into school. Dad's approach to this act of irresponsibility was so unexpected—and yet it was so needed. I wonder how different my life would be if he had not done what he did.

There are times in the life of a child when the consequences of his behavior are already built into the system. On those occasions, life itself serves up the punishment. Parents don't have to add to it. Lead with your heart at that point, not with your frustrations. Yes, I deserved a reprimand. At that point, however, it would have been like beating a dying man. What purpose would it have served?

These situations in life can be crucial to the growth of the child. They can also prove to be significant to the strengthening of the parent-child relationship. I expected to get a lecture and maybe even an additional consequence from my father. Since he had warned me so frequently, I deserved it. Instead, he chose to help me fight the battle.

I can't emphasize this point too much: Don't use a lecture to get personal relief from your child's failures. Use the opportunity to help growth take place. Therein lies a significant key to the overall concept of discipline and the parenting plan. Unfortunately, many parents choose to fight every single battle that comes along, and in doing so they lose the whole war. They seem to forget that it is the child's welfare that is of greatest concern. Instead, they take the child's behavior very personally and almost sit waiting for the failure so they can say "I told you so."

There is no doubt that I deserved to be lectured and punished. But the situation had a built-in punishment. Getting dismissed from college was in itself a very stiff consequence. My father assessed the situation and realized that he didn't need to add to that.

He took a different approach. He capitalized on the opportunity to be the one to lift me up in my time of need. It is significant to note that he wouldn't go do the difficult task for me. He wouldn't fly down to the dean's office and do the begging. In fact, he didn't even make the phone call. But he helped me have the courage to do the job myself.

Instead of lecturing me about what I had done wrong, Dad gave me an opportunity to do something right. That way I had a great feeling of victory when the dean told me I could have another chance, and the first person I wanted to tell was the person who had jumped on my team—Dad. Due to his very wise analysis of the situation, this was the beginning of the healing of our relationship.

Punishment Enough

Parents must keep in mind that the end result of discipline is a child's growth toward maturity—not the perverse gratification of being able to give the last "How many times do I have to tell you?" or "When will you ever learn?" The desired result should be a child who has the courage to push on to overcome the obstacle he faces. And that stands a better chance of happening if parents stay on the child's team.

Robey had spent the better part of a year saving his allowance. He was seven years old at the time and had been able to save twenty-four dollars at a dollar a week. This was a big deal, and it was about to get even better. It was April, and in June we were going on vacation. Our vacation tradition was that Dad would match whatever money each child had been able to save by the day we left. They used this as their spending money while we were away for the two weeks. If Robey didn't save another penny, his current savings meant he would have forty-eight dollars. This was an amazing amount of money for a seven-year-old, and he was very proud of his feat.

We were going to visit one of his cousins one Saturday that April. As we went out the door, I noticed that he had his wallet with him. "Why do you have your wallet, Robey?" I asked him. "We won't be going anywhere that you can buy anything."

"I know, Dad. I just want to show Wade how much money I have saved for this year's vacation," was his answer.

Wade was Robey's older cousin. Being a few years older meant Wade could do everything that Robey was not yet coordinated enough to do. I assume that he thought he would show off his twenty-four dollars.

"Robey, that's a very dangerous thing to do. You've worked hard at saving that money. Why risk losing it at Wade's house?" I questioned.

"I won't lose it, Dad. I'll be very careful with it. Please let me take my money to Wade's," he answered.

I decided to let him take his money and forgot about it. Later that night when we were back home, he asked his mom to stay in his bedroom after our prayers. It was obvious that he was waiting for me to leave. I was hurt, but I left them alone.

A few minutes later my wife, Rosemary, came out of his room and into the den. "What was that all about?" I asked.

She then told me a story that broke my heart. "The minute you left the room, Bob, Robey burst into tears. He said that he had taken his money to Wade's house and lost it."

At that point I was so upset that I started to get out of the chair and do what came naturally—go lecture him.

Rosemary stopped me and said, "Wait a minute; there's more. When I asked him why he didn't want you in the room, Bob, Robey said that he didn't want to tell you because you would only get mad and give him a lecture. He said that losing all his money was bad enough. He didn't want to upset you also."

I was devastated by the idea that my son might think of me as an uncompassionate ogre who always gives lectures, a father that he can't come to with problems, someone who is unbending and uncaring.

It was a great lesson for me. There are times when the situation itself carries punishment enough. Those times really offer a parent a golden opportunity to jump on the child's team and show compassion.

The Hinkley family did that when their son shot the president. They taught the whole viewing world what it meant for loving parents not to add to their child's difficulties. They couldn't pay his penalty for him any more than I should have reimbursed Robey for his lost money. They got on his team and did all they could to help.

P.S. Robey later found his wallet and money.

Summary

When your child has done something that has caused him to step over the boundaries that parent and child have previously discussed, the following procedure will be helpful:

1. Evaluate the situation. Does the behavior already carry with it a consequence apart from any consequence administered from the parent?

2. If the answer is no, the parent will need to proceed with the discipline plan that has already been established.

3. If the behavior does carry its own consequence, the question to be answered is: How can I best help my child at this point?

4. Establish a plan to help the child without taking away the consequence or its accompanying responsibilities.

5. Be an encourager.

19

Sibling Rivalry

IT'S 5:30 P.M.; MRS. JONES is doing everything she can to get ready for dinner. She is exhausted, and the kids are flying around the house with unending energy. Not being able to distract her from her kitchen responsibilities, they try a different game. It's called, "Let's Drive Mom Crazy."

Six-year-old Billy has a truck in the den that he has been playing with. His older brother, Eddie, decides that it would be fun to have that truck himself. Eddie has never shown an interest in the truck before now, but it has become more interesting since Billy currently seems to be enjoying it. All of a sudden there is pandemonium in the den. Mrs. Jones enters the room to find Eddie holding Billy's truck up in the air so that the younger child can't reach it. Little Billy screams in exasperation.

No Disciplinary Plan

Mrs. Jones is exhausted after her busy day and really can't believe that her children would pick this time of day to act like children. At this point, having no disciplinary plan, this mother sees only three ways to deal with the situation. First, she yells and screams at the children, warning them about what will happen if they continue this fighting.

Once she makes her threats, Mrs. Jones storms out of the room, but three minutes later she is shocked to find herself back in the den giving the same lecture again. This time the younger child is blackmailing the older one by crying as if he is being killed.

Mrs. Jones, in her desperation, decides to try a second course of action—the guilt approach. "How could you do this to me now? Don't you know what kind of day I've had?" she wails.

This approach will only cause the boys to escalate their attacks because no one has taken charge and no boundaries have been set. Therefore, the older one will do more antagonizing and the younger one will do more tattling. Mom will do more yelling and threatening, and end up with a headache. All of this continues because everyone in this scenario is looking to the next person to set the boundaries.

In a third attempt to deal with this case of sibling rivalry, Mrs. Jones appeals to the boys' intelligence. She may try to be very calm as she sits her boys down and talks to them about the importance of brotherly love. "Don't you know that you two need to take care of each other?" she asks. "If you don't protect each other, who else will?" That particular conversation may last for quite a while. But as soon as Mom leaves the room, the boys are at it again. In this case, Mom was counting on her teaching abilities to help the boys stop killing each other. The problem is much deeper than that, however. The children need to be seen for what they are. They are still only children, not mature enough to see the wisdom of treating each other with brotherly love.

Causes of Sibling Rivalry

What causes sibling rivalry? One answer is that it's just a natural part of family life. Living in a family offers a child an opportunity to live in a little "practice" society for a few years before he grows up and moves out into the real world. The family setting offers learning experiences in dealing with other people. Sibling rivalry is an important part of those learning experiences. Quite often, sibling rivalry is not just a behavior; it is a statement that the children want parental attention and response. There are many things going on in a child's life that he doesn't know how to discuss. Instead of *asking* parents to pay attention to him, he may choose to behave in a way that forces parental response.

Some children, especially the older children, feel like their key position of "only child" has been usurped by a younger sibling. It's as if they are saying, "Do you remember when it was only me, Mom? Those were the days. I really felt special then. We played together, and all the toys were mine. You were my best friend back then, Mom. But now Billy's here. Am I still your best friend, Mom? Am I still special? Show me, Mom."

Sibling rivalry is often an attempt at manipulating the parent to take sides. As soon as the younger child sees that the older child has been successful in that manipulation, the younger child will quickly enter the contest. His approach will likely be to tattle on the older one. Some children use this sibling combat to do little more than get a parent's attention. Their behavior says, "We've done everything else we can think of to get your attention, Mom. We've tried to talk to you about one of your favorite topics, the things that went on in school today—and all you had to say was 'Not right now.' Negative attention is better than no attention at all. Maybe if we kill each other we'll have your attention."

Obviously children aren't able to consciously think these approaches through, but they certainly learn how to get a parent's attention. Often that is all they want, and their misbehavior is to say, "If you would just come and sit with us for five minutes and let us each talk, we'd feel a lot better." Children are very jealous of anyone else getting their parent's attention. That's why they seem to act the wildest when Mom gets on the phone. "Hey, what about us, Mom? If you've got time for the phone, then you could certainly spend time with us," their behavior says.

What to Do—a Simple Plan

Sibling rivalry also can be seen as a challenge to a parent's authority, as well as a grasping for attention. It needs to be handled carefully. The response to this behavior must be handled objectively, and the hidden request of the children for time and attention must be met.

The behavior, on the other hand, must also be dealt with as unacceptable. The plan for dealing with this behavior must be simple enough for the child to understand, and the parent must announce the consequence. Then the parent must get out of the way and prepare to objectively enforce that consequence when the behavior occurs again.

The mother discussed here could have saved herself considerable frustration by using such a plan. "Eddie and Billy," she could start, "I want you to pay very close attention to me so that no one misunderstands." That way she can avoid having to respond to statements like, "But Mom, I didn't hear you!" Next she must define the unacceptable behavior: "The next time you two bother each other, tease each other, take something from each other, or touch each other, I will come back into the room and there will be a consequence." Mom may want to ask if there are any questions about what any of those things mean before she goes on to announcing what the consequence will be.

"If I have to come back into the den to referee, you will both be sent to sit in a chair. Billy, you will go to the dining room to sit in the chair you sit in at dinner. Eddie, you will go to sit in the blue chair on the porch.

"I will set this timer here in the kitchen, and you will both sit in your chairs with nothing to read or play with for fifteen minutes. At the end of that time, when the buzzer goes off, and not before, you can get up and go back to playing in the den. If you fight or argue again in the den, I will return you to your seats.

"One more thing I want to say about sitting in the chair is that while you are there, please don't ask me if you can get up now or if the time is up. You must learn to wait for the buzzer. If you get out of your chair beforehand or make any noise, including asking if you can get up, I will start the timer over again. Do you have any questions?"

Generally the children won't have any questions because they never dream that any of this will actually happen. A smart mom will then walk out of the den. She will walk out knowing, however, that she will be back in with the timer momentarily.

After a few minutes when what the children perceive as only an idle lecture wears off, they will probably be back at teasing each other again. It will be important for Mom to come back and calmly enforce what she said. She should not spend any time at this point listening to excuses or accusations. She should escort them to their chairs and turn on the timer. She may need to interrupt the children by adding, "I will start the timer when you are both quiet."

In a few minutes this parent will also need to be prepared to hear the words, "Isn't it time for the buzzer to go off yet, Mom?"

To this she should respond with, "Oh, no! I can't believe you talked! Now I have to start the timer all over again!"

A wise mom will also want to watch for games being played during this time in the chair. Fifteen minutes in a chair will not be as difficult for the older child as it will be for the younger one. It fact, it might be worth the wait to the older one just to know that his younger brother is also having to sit there. The older child may even use it as an opportunity to cause the younger to get more frustrated.

One mother told me that she caught her older child asking, on purpose, if it was time to get up yet. The boy said something like, "Is it time to get up yet, Mom? Oh, no. Now you have to start the timer over, don't you?"

This mom said it was so obvious that it was hilarious. Her response to this manipulation was, "Yes, I do have to start it over for you; but since your younger brother didn't say anything, he can get up now." She said that her older son never tried it again. The objective here is to deal with the behavior, while analyzing what the children are trying to say by acting in such a manner.

Analyze Their Behavior

While waiting for the buzzer to go off, Mom also has a chance to reflect on what the children's misbehavior is telling her. Perhaps it is saying that the children have been cooped up all day at school and they have a need to do something active. After they have successfully completed their fifteen minutes, Mom might want to take a break from her evening duties and do something with the children. This will certainly cause dinner to be late, but it will enrich the family, and it may also defuse the bickering.

There are times when arguing children can be forced to sit across a table from each other and talk. Perhaps they are arguing about what game to play or what to watch on television. This is an ideal opportunity to let them practice skills in negotiation. They should be told to sit down and discuss the problem until both are satisfied with a common solution. Parents should ask them what decision they have made and make sure that they are happy with the results. That will ensure that the older one has not intimidated the younger one.

Sibling rivalry can be at its worst during vacation travels. In fact, for many families the back-seat bickering can be a vacation wrecker. Parents can do several things to help with this problem, beginning with the realization that extended travel is difficult for children.

Many dads try to pack everyone in the car and travel "marathon" fashion. These dads would like to take no stops except for bathroom breaks, and they would like to do that while the engine is still running! Children cannot handle that pace unless they're anesthetized. Not only is it unfair and unpleasant to them, but it is also unwise. It only encourages boredom and back-seat fighting. Frequent stops to walk and eat can be very helpful. Switching seats after each stop will also help. Children can take turns sitting in the front seat and at the same time begin to learn how to read a map.

Rules need to be established. There is no way to avoid back-seat bickering without using the same discipline plan we've already discussed. Decide upon a consequence for the behavior, then stick with it. If a parent does nothing but threaten, yell, and scream, the time will very quickly come when a parent will do one other thing: dread vacation time.

Sibling rivalry and all its forms of expression offer great opportunities for learning. By learning how to deal with other people in the family, a child will be learning skills that will help him the rest of his life. So it's very important, for the future success of the child, that the parent develop a plan and stick with it.

Encourage Positive Action

On the positive side, there are things parents can do to help their children get along better. Perhaps the most significant is to set up situations that allow them to do things *for* each other rather than *to* each other. A sister could make cookies for the family. In the process, she could be encouraged to make a big special cookie for her brother. If he's a little boy, she could cut the cookie out in a special shape that would be appealing to him, such as an army tank or an animal.

When the daughter presents the cookie to her younger brother, it is important that the parents give the daughter tremendous feedback. "Look at that cookie Linda made for you, Bobby. Doesn't it make you feel good to know that your sister went to all the trouble to make something just for you? I'll tell you what, it sure makes me feel good. Thanks, Linda. That was a wonderful thing to do."

Perhaps there are other things Bobby could be encouraged to do for his sister. When he does them, however, the whole world needs to be notified. Both children must hear how happy everybody is when they do positive things for each other.

A few years ago, my son washed his bike while I was working at my workbench. When he finished, he asked me if I wanted him to wash my car. Actually what he was doing was having fun with a new hose nozzle. The car had very recently been washed, so I suggested that he wash his sister's bike instead.

"Why?" was his very honest response.

"Because it would be a nice thing to do for your sister," I said to him.

He went ahead and washed the bike, and when he was done, I went and got both Torrey and my wife, Rosemary. When they were all there, I said, "Look what Robey did." My daughter responded, "What did he do, break my bike?"

I was somewhat frustrated with her response, but Rosemary picked right up on what was going on. She began to praise Robey for going out of his way to help a family member. As the two of us stood there acting so positive, it wasn't long before Torrey started to say some nice things to her brother. She listened to the adults and realized it was a mature thing to do. Not only did the two children say nice things to each other that day, but Robey felt so good about his family membership that he volunteered to wash everything in sight.

Parents can jump to the offensive by encouraging the children to do nice things for each other. And when these nice things are done, the parent must see to it that there is a proper response from the other child. Teach them to say positive things to each other and to serve each other, and they won't have to be in constant competition with each other.

Summary

When dealing with sibling rivalry, it is important to note that it will usually occur when you have the least patience or time to deal with it. So decide ahead of time what you will do the next time you must confront sibling rivalry, and avoid letting personal frustration be your guide.

1. Define for your children the behavior that is unacceptable.

2. Establish the consequence that will be administered if they continue this behavior after you leave the room.

3. Leave the room. But don't think you have solved the problem by giving your lecture. Leave the room with the understanding that you will probably be back. Because the children are bad and rebellious? No! Because they are children.

4. Analyze what, if anything, the children are trying to tell you with their behavior. This does not negate the consequence for their behavior, but it may say that they need the parent to spend more time with them.

5. Establish ways your children can show acts of kindness to each other.

6. When they are doing a good job of getting along, let them know how good it makes you feel.

PART VI

Maturity: Postponing a Present Desire for a Future Benefit

20

A Plan for Teaching Self-Control

FAR TOO OFTEN discipline is seen only as a reaction to a negative behavior. In that case we see the parental job of discipline as little more than adults waiting to pounce on misbehaving children. In a home such as that, children might learn what *not* to do, but they would never learn the positive actions to take to become mature adults.

A parental plan for discipline must jump to the offense. A football team that only has a defense will never score. Many parents in today's world spend all their efforts concentrating on the defense and never get to the offense.

Parents must have a plan to help children prepare for the future and acquire the many skills they will need as adults. For example, children must be helped to learn self-control and personal discipline. And they must be taught there is no such thing as situation ethics. Ethics, and the decisions concerning them, are always the same, regardless of the situation at hand.

One way to help children begin to learn these lessons of life is by looking at the lives of the patriarchs. The account of Joseph's life in Scripture provides a great example of self-control and personal discipline under a wide variety of circumstances. One bad thing after another happened to Joseph. Perhaps the final straw was the fact that Potiphar's wife was after him. She wanted him to commit adultery with her, and even though she and her husband owned Joseph, he refused to give in to her.

Many times teen-agers attempt to justify their decisions by saying everyone would laugh at them if they actually did the things they knew were right. "But Mom, if I had walked out of that party when they brought out the beer, I would have been the laughingstock of the high school," they protest. Parents know that these fears are not really true and that others at the party would probably have been encouraged by one teen-ager being so bold. Nevertheless, a teen-ager does not yet know that. Stories such as Joseph's help the young person put it all into perspective. They can see that sometimes it does cost to do the things that are right, but the cost can pay off later in life.

"Son, do you think that Joseph had to deal with being embarrassed when he walked out of Potiphar's wife's "party"? Worse than being embarrassed, he had to go to jail for many years."

Personal Discipline

Personal discipline is displayed by one who has been taught to control his own desires. Such discipline seems rare in our society. A friend of mine who leads Bible studies commented to me about how hard it was to get people today to commit to ten straight weeks of early-morning study. "The lack of personal discipline is amazing," my friend said. "Business men call me and ask to be a part of one of my Bible study groups. They say that they are serious about their spiritual growth. Then when I tell them that the Bible study group meets on Tuesday mornings at 7:00 A.M., it's amazing how their enthusiasm starts to fade. The enthusiasm leaves many of them totally when I say that they must commit to be present ten in a row." Many of these men actually respond to my friend with, "I don't know if I can commit to get up that early for ten straight Tuesdays."

Our society today seems to find it difficult to commit sacrificially to anything or anyone. Unfortunately, without the personal discipline to make and keep commitments of this nature, our children will miss out on the most important thing there is—God's plan for their life.

Just as God planted the trees in the soils and climates that are the right locations to perform their proper ecological tasks, it should be equally obvious that He has a special plan for each of our children. Without the ability to be personally disciplined, they will lack the ability to stay pure, to study to find God's will, or to dig in and do God's work.

Everyone's natural reaction is to respond to his own impulse. It's a relief when we mature enough to find out that we don't have to respond to all of our urges. Children can be taught that they are not slaves to their bodies or their desires. A mature, disciplined person can force his body to respond to his will.

Joseph was able to do just that. He was able to control his body and take a stand for the things that were right before God. Yes, he did suffer for a while for his stand. In the long run, however, he reaped the benefits of placing his life in God's hands. Joseph went from a slave in prison to being the Prime Minister of Egypt. He reached this high position because he was able to control himself regardless of the circumstances.

The next four chapters will be concerned with maturity and the personal discipline that parents must teach their children so they will be able to respond to life in a mature manner. These are lessons that require a plan so that the children can respond properly to the challenges life puts before them.

Summary

1. Self-control doesn't just come with age. It is a lesson that must be taught to each child.

2. Children can begin to learn about self-control by studying the lives of those that have gone before us.

3. Part of self-control training is to learn not to respond to urges.

4. Sometimes self-control means short-term suffering for long-term good.

21

The Discipline of Financial Stewardship

STATISTICS TELL US that the inability to handle money, and conflict over finances, is one of the leading causes of divorce in our society. Isn't it amazing that something that is a blessing in our country, the financial resources available to us, can so easily be a curse?

Most young couples are totally unprepared to deal with the money they will be responsible to handle. Many are unprepared because they never had the opportunity or responsibility to handle any money when they were young. Just as surely as children need to eat their vegetables, children also need to be responsible for money of their own. This opportunity to handle and be responsible for money can best come in the form of an allowance. Allowances, handled properly, can be a great help for teaching children financial discipline.

When I was a boy, starting at about four years old, I received an allowance, as did everyone in the Barnes household. After we were old enough to write, Dad even had us make out a financial request form. Sometime before Christmas we would each write down what allowance we wanted for the next year and why. Then before New Year's Day he would call us up to his study, and we would defend our request. It was a horrible experience! I remember being nervous as I walked up the stairs for my turn at Dad's "interrogation." My little brother would go first, and I would pass him on the stairs after he had finished his session with Dad. He always looked sweaty when he came out of Dad's study!

We would always get what we asked for. That was probably because we were too scared to ask for much! Actually, it was a very valuable time of Dad teaching us about the seriousness of money. I can remember him saying, "If you don't put money in its proper perspective, Son, it can ruin your life." He wanted his boys to be disciplined in the handling of money so that money didn't end up handling them.

When I was older, I remember getting a dollar allowance each week. My father handled it in a very professional manner. We would be given our money on Fridays, and it was ours to do with as we pleased. I generally got on my bicycle and rode to a store to purchase baseball cards—as many as my dollar would buy. It was great riding home with a large mass of baseball bubblegum in my mouth and looking through my new cards. (I didn't need my hands to guide the bike.) It was great—until the next morning, anyway. A friend would come over and ask us if we wanted to go to the skating rink with him.

"Sure, I can go," I would say. "Just wait a minute while I ask my dad." What I was really doing was asking my dad for a loan, since I had already spent my money. His response was always the same, "Bob, I'm not a savings and loan institution." After a while I realized that he wasn't going to loan me any money. If I wanted any of the finer opportunities in life, like skating at the rink, I was going to have to get disciplined in the handling of my money.

In years past if an adult spent all his money he would have to wait until the next payday. The system itself was enough to discipline people in the handling of their finances. Unfortunately, it's not that way anymore. Our culture today encourages young adults to have whatever they want, when they want it. Don't wait until you can afford it, just charge it. The credit system in our society feeds the material lust of young adults. It also can cause their downfall as they are forced to spend their lives trying to pay off debt. Many families are forced to send every able-bodied adult in the home, including older teen-agers, out into the work force.

Dad's consistent, unbending way of training his boys about money has been extremely beneficial now that we are adults. In order to help children grow up to be disciplined in the handling of their finances, there must be a parenting plan.

Be Consistent with Allowance

The child must be given some money in order to learn how to handle money. This means giving a consistent amount of money the same day every week, just as a paycheck is handled. Some parents believe they can't afford to give a child a consistent amount of money every week. They give the child money one week, and then they can't do it the next week because they themselves are not financially disciplined. The child learns to beg for money and the parent feels guilty. In this situation, when the parent has money in the weeks to come he ends up giving the child more than he should because of feeling guilty.

This kind of financial plan doesn't teach a child how to handle money. Instead, it really teaches a child how to beg a parent to give in. Once again we see a disciplinary plan that puts the responsibility on the wrong shoulders, with the parent holding responsibility for deciding whether to give in and give more money. When this happens the child has no responsibility at all.

The amount of money given as an allowance is not the significant factor here. In fact, I would venture to guess that the parent who believes he really can't afford a consistent allowance would be surprised to know how much he actually hands out by the end of a year. If that parent kept track of the money he sporadically gave to the child out of guilt, he would probably find it to be a greater amount than if it were done in a consistent allowance form.

Let the Allowance Be Theirs

When Robey turned four, we started giving him one dollar a week. We wanted him to have the opportunity to spend his own money. He very quickly learned that this was a great medium of exchange. And even though we talked to him about saving his money to purchase bigger things, money seemed to burn a hole in his little pocket.

Finally Robey saved over three dollars, all in dimes. He was begging to go to a big toy store to spend his money, and I was very disappointed that he wanted to spend it. I guess I thought that my talks on finances would motivate this little boy to start saving for his retirement. As Robey and I went out the door of our house, headed for the toy store, Rosemary stopped me and sweetly said, "Bob, let him spend his own money. Don't buy it for him." *Of course, Dear,* I thought. *What else were these lessons for?*

When we got to the store it was a different story, however. Robey went right to the G.I. Joe section to pick out a soldier. He had already been told that even though it was his money and he could buy whatever he could afford, there were certain toys that he would not be permitted to purchase. G.I. Joes were on the okay list, and he had just enough money to buy one. Robey sat down on the floor in front of the rack of G.I. Joes and pulled out four of the soldiers, agonizing over which one to buy. Finally he looked up at me and said, "Daddy, I can't decide which one to get. Could you buy all four for me?"

The temptation was absolutely unbelievable. For only twelve dollars I could be a hero for my little boy! If only Rosemary hadn't made that statement to bring me back on track! But we were giving him an allowance to help him learn how to make money decisions, and buying those four soldiers for him would have defeated our whole purpose—not to mention it would have made it impossible to face the woman I love!

"No, Robey," I began. "You're going to have to decide for yourself. Buy the one you want the most and save your money to buy another later."

Robey made his decision and carried his G.I. Joe up to the cash register. He pulled out his little wallet and counted out the money, dime by dime, as I announced to the cashier what was probably obvious—that he was making this purchase with his own money.

Robey was proud of his purchase. And I soon noticed a major difference with letting him buy things with his own money. That night when he was in bed, I did not find his new G.I. Joe on the ground in the backyard. Instead, as I looked at him asleep in bed, I found the new toy on his pillow, embedded in the side of his little face. He had paid for it, so he wasn't going to lose it.

Let them have the money—and then let them spend it, even on things you consider a waste. When you take a child to the grocery store, for example, there is a strategic opportunity for teaching financial discipline as they beg you for a coin for the inevitable "coin-trap machine." Children love to put a coin in them so they can twist a handle and get some kind of green glob that they lose in the parking lot. The machines are strategically placed by the doors so children will beg when you have your arms filled with bags, with your change still clutched in your hand. Most parents are too embarrassed to argue with their children in front of all the other shoppers. So they grudgingly give in and give the children a quarter.

The next time your children want money for these machines, help them learn the value of that coin by making them use their own money. As we walked out of a store one day, my daughter asked, "Daddy, could I have one of those?" I responded with, "Sure, Honey. Your purse is in the car. Let's get it, and I'll walk back in here with you so you can buy it with your money." When we got to the car, she never mentioned it again. It was worth my money—but obviously not worth her own.

Let them spend their money so that they learn the discipline involved in spending decisions. Children will fail many times with money and spend their hard-earned savings foolishly. I would rather give them the opportunity to fail with their money while they are children, though, than fail when they get their first paycheck.

Many young adults have never been personally responsible for their own money. Then all of a sudden they leave home and earn their first check. Since they have never developed personal discipline in the area of finances, they are apt to begin making purchases that are way over their heads.

Teach Them about Credit

It is the parent's responsibility to help children understand money, and part of that lesson in today's world includes an understanding of credit. "Oh, you've got to be kidding," one parent blurted out during a seminar when I mentioned this topic. "There is no way that my child could ever handle credit!" That is exactly the point. Someday each child will have to know how to handle credit, or it will handle him. That's why children in today's world must be given the opportunity to experience the use of credit before they leave home.

There are many ways to teach teen-agers about handling credit, but few are more creative than the plan of one mom I recently read about. One summer this particular mom decided to issue each of her children a "Parent Card." This was a credit card that she made up and actually went to the trouble of having covered with plastic. She issued one to each of her three teen-agers and explained the system to them. Each child was given a credit limit according to what she felt they could make per month. The oldest child was seventeen and working in a store part-time, so he was given a credit limit of two hundred dollars. The youngest child was cutting lawns and thus given a credit limit of forty dollars.

The mom explained to her children that the cards would be handled just like regular credit cards. "When I am with you at a store and you see something that you want, come and get me. I will let you use your Parent Card. That means that I will buy it for you and then give you a receipt. At the end of each week you must pay 25 percent of your balance, plus 10 percent interest. The Friday that you are unable to do that, you lose your card for a month and will not get it back until you have paid your whole balance."

She said that her teen-agers were ecstatic. The first time they went to a store one of them ran up to her with an item and asked, "Mom, can I charge it on my Parent Card?" "Certainly you can, Honey," the mom responded. "Just let me have your card."

The teen-ager looked a little puzzled. "But, Mom," he gasped, "I left it at home. Won't it be okay to charge if I left it at home?" This mom responded with, "Do you think the store clerk would say it was okay if I told her that I left my credit card at home but I would like to charge something anyway? We said this was going to be handled just like a credit card, and that means you must have the card with you to get the credit."

After a week of excitement for the children when they could get lots of things without paying cash for them, they faced another reality. It was time to pay 25 percent plus the interest. The children could hardly believe that they had to pay interest. "This just isn't fair," the youngest one cried. "I don't understand why I should pay money that I didn't use. Interest isn't fair!"

This whole experience was a great lesson in self-control. By the end of the summer the two oldest children weren't even using their credit cards anymore. The newness had worn off, and they were learning the discipline of delayed gratification.

Teach Them to Budget Money

When children are older, during high school, they can also be given the opportunity to handle a budget. If a teen-ager's total expenses are seventy-five dollars a month after totaling up school lunches, toiletries, etc., sit down with them and let them handle it.

"Eddie," one father started, "you have been buying lunches every day, and I have been giving you the money at the beginning of each week. That expense, as well as some of the other items you have needed, such as gas money for our car, total about seventy-five dollars each month. I have decided that I'm not going to force you to come to me for every little item. From now on, I am going to give you seventy-five dollars at the beginning of each month, and that amount must last you until the first of the next month. Do you have any questions?"

This particular father said that two very interesting things happened. The first was that his son got right up and went to his room to try and recalculate his monthly expenses. "Dad, can I talk to you about the budget?" Eddie asked. "When I try to figure out my expenses here on this paper, it seems that they are more like eighty dollars a month." The father was happy with the fact that his son seemed to take this exercise seriously.

The second thing that happened was even more exciting. Eddie did something that in the past was beneath him. He began to buy his own supplies and bring sack lunches from home rather than buy lunch at school. He had calculated that the sack lunches would be cheaper. The lesson of learning to budget was working.

Certainly the teen-ager will fail. But now, while he is still at home, is the perfect time to fail. It's too difficult to know how to help when he is out on his own and has overextended himself.

The Question of Chores

As can be seen by other statements in this book, I do believe that every child should have family chores to do. It is my opinion, however, that there should not be a connection between the chores and the allowance. Children should not be paid to be a working member of the family. No one gives Dad extra money to wash the cars. He does it because it is a responsible thing for a family member to do.

Many parents get themselves to the point where they ask a child to do something and he responds with, "How much will I get?" Some parents have worked up a payment chart for the child's family chores. If the child does the dishes, he gets fifty cents, and if he takes out the garbage, he gets thirty cents. As the child gets older, that amount of money is much less significant. "Mom, I don't want to take out the garbage for thirty cents anymore. Bring in hired help to do it for that amount!" one might argue.

I do believe that a child may hit a point when he will receive no allowance at all because he is not functioning as a family member. In this way the allowance can be construed as being connected to the chores. When he doesn't do anything that a family member is expected to do, then he should not get any of the family privileges, such as an allowance.

I also believe that there are extra chores, above and beyond the child's normal responsibilities, that the child can be paid for if he wants to earn more money. Those extra chores, or financial opportunities, can be written up on a board with the amount of money to be paid next to it. That way the child can choose to make a little extra money.

No one should get paid to be a member of a family, however. And that membership means that there are responsibilities to be performed.

Teach Them to Tithe

We started our children with an allowance of one dollar, given in dimes. This particular monetary denomination was chosen for a purpose. When I first became a Christian, I was a young adult. The obedient financial response of tithing was initially unbearable. I decided to tithe, but I certainly wasn't going to like it. What it boiled down to was the fact that I couldn't decide which I trusted more, my money or my Lord. I hadn't received the training for this commitment when I was a child.

I don't want my children to grow up with that dilemma. I want them to know the joy of tithing long before they reach adulthood. The only way a child can know that joy, however, is to have something of his own to give; his offering should come from his allowance. I asked the church I attend to give each of my children their own offering envelopes. Now the offering time has become a special part of the service for my children. They aren't putting a quarter in the plate that Dad gave them before the service.

When our children were little, they were permitted to draw in church during the service. There was only one rule about drawing. They had to include in their picture something that pertained to the sermon. This often meant that Robey would first draw a cross, to get his obligation out of the way. Then he would fill his picture with tanks and airplanes zooming around the cross. The offering time was different, however. When the ushers came down the aisle for the offering, Robey would put his drawing book down and search his pockets for his wadded-up offering envelope. When he found the envelope, he would quickly straighten it out on a hymnal and wait patiently for the offering plate to come to him. He was not only proud to be able to place his offering in the plate, he was also full of joy.

Perhaps the most significant part of financial discipline is understanding that the Lord is more capable than any amount of money. As parents, by placing our faith in God above our faith in money, we will help our children learn who it is they can trust.

Summary

It is very significant that children be taught financial discipline. In order for a child to become mature about handling money, his parents must institute a training plan. That can be done through an allowance.

1. Give a child an allowance, starting when they are about four or five years old.

2. The same amount of money should be handed out consistently each week.

3. The parent should allow the child to experience spending his own money.

4. Parents must also plan to teach their children about the use of credit.

5. Children must be taught the obedience and joy of tithing with their own money.

22

The Discipline of Patience

"BUT DAD, HOW MUCH longer are we going to be working on this boat?" fourteen-year-old Michael pleaded with his father. "I'm tired of spending all this time sanding and painting." For what seemed like the tenth time, Michael's father repeated the same statement. "If you want to receive a share of the benefits of the sale of this old boat, you are going to have to be willing to be patient as the whole family works together."

Patience. What a key word in today's society. Where are those people who have the ability to endure and wait? Are we raising any more Edisons who have the discipline to stick with a project for months, weeks, or even hours, until success is achieved? That kind of maturity takes practice. It takes growing up in a home that includes the discipline of patience in the parenting plan.

Is it really that important? Patience is the maturity that will help a young adult stick to his educational goals without getting discouraged and dropping out. Patience is the discipline necessary in a career that will help a young employee work hard toward a goal or benefits that may be a decade away. And certainly the ability to respond with patience will be mandatory in the marriage relationship. Patience will also be a very special quality while spending eighteen years rearing children. Is the discipline of patience really important? Only to those parents who want their children to find success in areas such as education, profession, marriage, and family.

The discipline of patience is never more significant than in a child's growth in his faith. Patience is the ingredient that will help a child, and eventually an adult, have the ability to wait on the Lord as He answers prayers and needs in His own perfect timing. Many adults miss God's perfect plan because they lack the discipline of patience. Patience is not a part of maturity that comes suddenly when a child becomes an adult.

Nor is it a maturity that some of us have and some of us don't have, and no one knows why. It is a discipline that parents must nurture as their children grow up.

In years past, planning to teach children about patience was not necessary. The culture itself did the job very nicely. Many children grew up on a farm where the very nature of the growth cycle of crops or animals taught patience. Many who did not grow up on farms were apprenticed under a tradesman and waited patiently for years for an opportunity to work at that trade on their own. Children then grew up automatically experiencing the precepts of patience. It was so evident in day-to-day life that parents probably thought little about training a child in this particular discipline.

Life in America is very different today. Even my grandmother, who lives in southern Germany, noticed the lack of patience in the American attitude. Several years ago when I was moving from an apartment to a house, I was trying to get the phone company to transfer my phone service from one location to the other. I was very exasperated that they would not be able to do it all in one day. My grandmother, when she heard of my situation, very quickly chided me for my pathetic lack of patience. Apparently in my grandmother's part of the German Alps, the wait for phones is approximately two years. When it recently got to be her turn for a phone, she gave the privilege away to one of her children and put her name back on the bottom of the list to wait for another two years!

The very essence of modern American society teaches young people that all things can be done instantly. The television shows they watch teach them that overwhelming problems can be solved in about an hour. Another example of this lack of patience is shown by our buying habits. As we've already discussed, the predominate attitude here is "if you see something you want, don't wait and save to purchase it—just charge it."

Sexual purity until marriage is another example of patience. Some materials being handed out to our children no longer show a reason for this patience. Instead of abstinence, the young people are being told to use some form of birth control. Why wait when you can be sexually active without getting yourself into trouble? That deceptive mentality, that "have-it-now" thinking, has permeated all areas of our society. Why should parents train their children and young people in the discipline of patience? Because it will help them save themselves, not only from the temptations of life, but also for the purpose in which they were created. Patience is the discipline that will stand them above the rest of the crowd. But they must have the opportunity to learn it, and that opportunity must be provided in the home.

Teaching Patience

Patience in the young child can be developed beginning with the toys they enjoy. Many toys for children today do all the work; the child does little more than watch and react. Toys such as plastic interlocking blocks or logs (Legos or Lincoln Logs), on the other hand, allow the child to create and teach a young child how to work toward a goal. Toys that allow a child the opportunity to fail, as he watches his tower of blocks fall down, for example, give him the experience of starting over and trying again until he reaches his goal. Toys that have step-by-step building or operating procedures will be more effective at enhancing his discipline of patience and perseverance than those toys that move by themselves while he simply watches.

Video toys and games usually do little for a child in the area of creativity. Though they may be a challenge that can be attacked repeatedly, they allow the child to remain for hours in a sedentary position, making very few long-term decisions. Instead, he reacts to a screen without thinking.

Teaching a child to love reading is another way to enhance patience. Children can learn the joy of reading a book even though it may take hours more than watching a movie or video. Families can further help by doing jigsaw puzzles together. Many of today's children have no idea what jigsaw puzzles are, let alone the reason to put one together.

A few years ago I put a jigsaw puzzle on a card table in the big living room of one of the homes for boys at Sheridan House. After putting a chair next to the table, I sat down one evening and began putting the one thousand pieces together. For the first few minutes the boys just walked by, giving me that look, as if to say, "What crazy thing is he doing now?" One of them even asked, "How long will that take to finish?" "Probably about four or five hours if no one helps me," I said. They walked away, as if to say, "Too long. Forget it!"

Fifteen minutes went by, and two boys were standing over my shoulder pointing out pieces. "See if it fits," I suggested. The next thing I knew three boys were sitting down, helping me. By the end of the week we had several tables set up with three or four boys at each, taking hours to put together jigsaw puzzles. I learned that the boys *could* get interested in such patience-teaching adventures as jigsaw puzzles. The key was that an adult was there to help them enter into the exercise so that they didn't have to start from scratch all alone.

Working on model airplanes or ships, as well as assembling and decorating a wooden dollhouse, are all exercises in patience. Fishing is a sport that will teach patience. Vegetable gardening is a hobby that will also teach patience as the child learns to watch for growth day after day. There are many other activities that will also force a child to develop discipline in this area, including hiking and camping as a family. Even the chore of starting a camp fire will teach patience.

A Time to Think

A byproduct that accompanies any exercise in patience is an opportunity for a child to have some time to actually think. For example, whether he is sitting on a river bank fishing or pulling weeds in a vegetable garden, he will have time to think about the things that are happening around him in life. Unfortunately, too many of a child's activities today rob him of that opportunity.

In 1974 I arrived at Sheridan House at the same time that Glen Reese was called to be minister of youth at a local church. Glen was single and he didn't have anywhere to live, so we offered him a room at Sheridan House. My first year in this ministry was very difficult, and due to the lack of a house parent, I spent many nights sleeping there rather than being able to go home. Many of those nights I stayed up into the early morning hours talking with Glen. It was so amazing to me how much wisdom this young man had. Finally I asked him one night, "Glen, when have you thought about all these things that we talk about? It's incredible to me that you seem to be so wise beyond your years. It's obvious that you have set aside time to think through many more decisions in life than I have."

Glen's answer was very simple, yet very profound. "I think that it's probably because of our different upbringing," Glen began. "You grew up in the city, Bob, where you were always doing things and running around with friends. I grew up in the country where I spent most afternoons after school sitting alone on my daddy's tractor, plowing up and down the fields. I had time to think about life, while you only had time to react to life's circumstances."

He was right. The exercises that teach patience also allow a child or young person an opportunity to think about life's decisions. Children's lives are usually so packed with events, lessons, and practice sessions parents have to purposefully decide to institute activities that teach this discipline. Otherwise, there's just no time left in a child's life to sit with a fishing pole. And that may mean there's no time or inclination to take the opportunity to think about life. Patience is not only a discipline, it's also a maturity that allows one the time to think through life rather than simply react like a bouncing pinball.

The first step, obviously, is for the parent to see the need and then make the decision to develop this discipline in the child. We all must be willing to acknowledge the fact that it will no longer just happen. Anyone who has been in line at a fast-food store knows that patience no longer comes with age. The elderly can be just as grumpy, when caused to wait, as the young. It is not an automatic discipline that comes with age. Patience is a form of maturity that parents must give their children the opportunity to learn.

The second step is to make wise choices as to the toys and activities the child will be involved in. What does this toy give the child an opportunity to learn? Is it simply a form of momentary entertainment, or does it enhance valuable skills? Some toys should be just for having fun. Other toys, however, can teach lessons that last a lifetime.

The third step for parents to take is to get involved in the play time of the child. This can help tremendously. Children will be more willing to practice patience if they have encouragement. Even games that are seemingly little more than amusement can be used to teach lessons, if the parent is willing to get involved and help the child see the lesson being illustrated.

Two summers ago I bought very sophisticated water guns for everyone in my family. I used the excuse that I wanted my children to experience some of the toys that I had fun with when I was a boy. My wife saw right through me, however. She knew I was just looking for a way to buy myself one of the new water guns. We divided up into teams and played a game of one team trying to find the other and then soaking them with the water.

Robey and I were on the same team, and we got to hide first. We looked for a place where we could surprise Torrey and her grandfather before they could get us. Robey and I finally hid in some tall ferns and waited. Our location must have been too good; it was fifteen minutes before the other two even came near us. Robey was dying of impatience. "Let's go get them, Dad," he said in desperation. "I don't want to wait anymore." It was all I could do to get him to stay hidden until they finally were within range. Then we attacked, soaked them down, and won the game.

After we were the obvious winners, with both Torrey and Grandpa looking pathetically soaked, little Robey began jumping up and down, shouting, "We won because we waited. We won because we waited." The fact that he was bragging about it told me that the waiting must have been a very difficult thing for him to do. He learned a lesson that day, however—not one that will last for life, but a lesson that can be used as a building block upon which to place other exercises in patience. Take advantage of every opportunity to teach and underline the discipline of patience in your child's life. It may mean the difference between failure and success in life's most important ventures.

Summary

1. Patience is a discipline that will help children stick with their goals in life. It will affect their education, marriage relationships, or anything that requires an effort.

2. Patience is very significant where one's faith is concerned.

3. Fun activities at home, such as puzzles and model airplanes, can build the discipline of patience.

4. Parents can make wise choices of toys and activities for their children that will build the discipline of patience.

23

The Discipline of Dealing with Peer Pressure

"BUT MOM, EVERYBODY ELSE has those! I just don't understand why you won't let me get a pair." Sound familiar? If you have children who are over ten years of age, no doubt you've heard those words many times. Peer pressure is a difficult area of life for young people and adults alike. If peer pressure is not dealt with in youth, it could be a very damaging factor in adulthood.

Peer pressure is like a monster that moves into the life of an individual. It slowly takes over the decision-making process until things may be done that make little or no sense—except that the person's peers are doing them. Peer pressure is a device our society uses to justify behavior that we know deep down inside is something we would be better off not doing—better off in the long run, anyway.

Peer pressure affects many areas of life, but perhaps the two most profound areas are one's personal moral code and the way one handles money. It takes discipline to be able to resist these temptations. Many children grow up in homes that do not allow them to see the reality of just what peer pressure is. Those children enter into adulthood still in the grips of peer pressure. Many of their most basic decisions are dictated not by their own desires, but rather by those of their peers.

Parents should not try to inhibit their children from having the opportunity to deal with peer pressure. Instead, they should help prepare their children for dealing with peer pressure by talking about it. Children must be made aware of how peer pressure can affect their decision making. Parents can do this by labeling peer pressure when it occurs and allowing time to discuss it with the children. Finally, parents must allow their children the opportunity to pay the price for succumbing to peer pressure when the consequences are not too severe.

Peer Pressure and Money

Nicole went shopping with her mother to purchase a pair of new jeans. Right from the beginning it became obvious that parent and child had different ideas about which jeans would be adequate. "Nicole," this mother started to explain, "you and I have a different opinion about which jeans we should buy for you. These jeans that I have picked out are very nice and cost twenty-two dollars. The jeans over there that you seem to want cost forty-one dollars. I will pay twenty-two dollars toward the purchase of those jeans for you if you want."

"But Mom, who will pay the rest of the money for the jeans?" Nicole responded, as if she didn't really know what was happening. "I don't understand. These jeans cost less than the jeans that you bought me for my birthday. Why won't you buy these for me now? It doesn't make sense."

"It makes a lot of sense," Nicole's mom answered. "That was your birthday, and I wanted to get you a special present that you wanted. This is different. We are just here to buy you some everyday jeans. You have money. This more expensive pair, that some of your friends are wearing, may be worth the family's money to you, but are they worth your own money? This is a purchase that you are wanting to make because of peer pressure. It is expensive to give into peer pressure. You decide which pair that you want."

This mother could have easily paid the price for the expensive jeans. Instead, she used it as an opportunity to help her daughter mature in the discipline of dealing with peer pressure. Not only did the mother make her daughter pay the difference, but she also labeled it for what it was. In that way the girl could better understand the real factors that were involved.

It was a wise move to let the girl have the jeans if she was willing to pay the difference. It's better for her to have the chance to fumble through those decisions as a child, rather than face them for the first time when she gets her first paycheck as an adult. Those are the times when many adults make incredibly expensive purchases that they spend years regretting. Many new cars are purchased on credit by young adults solely because it is "the in car to have" at the time.

Young people should be given the opportunity to find out the price of peer pressure while they still live at home. It may save them significant bills later on in life. Succumbing to peer pressure is an expensive behavior.

Peer Pressure and One's Moral Code

Peer pressure can also erode a young person's moral code. "I wouldn't have done it, Mom, but everyone else was doing it, and I didn't know how not to." A feeling of wanting to belong can cause a teen-ager to be very undisciplined in the handling of his behavior or body.

When I was in college, I went through a very difficult time in my life of feeling like I didn't belong to anything. Then I met and began dating a girl who let me know from our first date that she was a Christian. I was shocked at the fact that she seemed to know where she was going in life. It was such a contrast from what was happening in my own life. After dating for several weeks, I invited her up to a party my fraternity was having in a chalet in the mountains off our campus. She agreed to go but announced that she would not be spending the night. She had heard that some of the girls were going to be there all night, and she was not going to be one of them. I shrugged it off, thinking that she would change her mind once we got there. After all when she saw that everyone else was going to stay, I was sure she would feel too ridiculous being the only one to leave.

It was shortly before eleven that night that Rosemary announced she needed to be getting back to the dorm. "But Rosemary," I protested. "Everyone else is staying until tomorrow. Why don't you just stay?" It didn't do any good. She very sweetly told me that if I didn't drive her home, she would find a ride. As we got our things together to leave the chalet, an interesting thing happened. Three other girls gathered their belongings and asked me if they, too, could have a ride. Peer pressure had no effect on Rosemary, and the fact that she knew where she was going in life saved a few other girls from giving in to it that night, too.

As the years went on and we dated more and more seriously, I remember asking her how she was able to stay so pure and impervious to peer pressure. She was an interesting combination of sweet and fun to be with, yet strong in her convictions. Rosemary said that it all boiled down to a discipline of commitment. For years her parents had helped her develop the discipline to commit herself to lifetime goals and ideals, no matter what was happening around her.

Rosemary was committed to her family. And she knew that her family represented far more than the current generation. Her family members were very close and spent hours talking together. Ever since she was a little girl, she had been told about the previous generations on both parents' sides. The stories helped her feel as if she actually had met the people who had been dead long before she was born. In short, when Rosemary faced peers, she never felt isolated and alone because she had been reared to believe that she was a significant part of something special, a long line of family members that she represented.

To get this attitude across to their children, Rosemary's parents spent many pleasant hours telling stories about the family. Her grandparents also helped. Many of their vacations were geared around spending time with extended family members. This helped young Rosemary feel that she belonged to something special. She was taught loyalty to her parents and to the past generations.

Rosemary's mother also helped her develop a loyalty in another, very curious area. From childhood on, Rosemary was taught to be loyal to a husband she had not yet met, but who she would eventually spend her life with. This discipline of commitment was so frequently talked about and so real to Rosemary that she actually pictured anything that she might do to violate that loyalty as a betrayal. It was easier for her to walk out of that chalet because she was determined to be loyal to her future husband, whoever he was. It just so happened that I turned out to be that very fortunate man.

Rosemary's future husband was made more real to her because his qualities were discussed in those talks with her parents. This is an excellent idea for any parent: Help young people look at the qualities they want in a spouse at an early age. One friend helped his daughter write down the qualities that she wanted in a husband and keep the list in her Bible. Every now and then when they were out to dinner alone, this father would ask his daughter to bring her "Husband List" so they could go over it. "Now what are the qualities that you want your future husband to have?" this dad would ask. He did this to help make this future relationship more vivid and also to help her begin to picture the qualities she thought would be valuable. He wanted her to be able to look past a handsome face.

It turned out that this list helped him combat the peer pressure that surrounded his daughter's dating relationship with a young man. At the end of college Cathy came to her dad and said that Brian, the boy she had dated her senior year, had asked her to marry him. It seemed like the right thing to do. Her friends were getting married. Plus her friends were encouraging her to marry Brian. She wanted to know what her dad thought. "Let's go out to dinner tonight and discuss it," he responded. "And bring your 'Husband List.'"

Cathy's dad told me that as he and his daughter sat at dinner and read the list again, he asked, "Well, what do you think? Is this the man you have been waiting for?" Cathy burst into tears and said, "He's not the one, is he, Dad?"

This father was very grateful that he did not have to be the one to fight the peer pressure of a college sweetheart and the couple's friends. Instead, the strength to do the right thing was based in their parent-daughter relationship and the time they had spent in the past making Cathy's future husband a reality. Just like Cathy and Rosemary, any child, boy or girl, can stay loyal to a future spouse if a parent is willing to help it happen.

The discipline of dealing with peers includes one other necessary relationship of loyalty. Once again, Rosemary's parents illustrate exactly what I want to say. Besides being loyal to her parents and past generations, and to her future husband, above all else Rosemary was taught to be loyal to her Lord. Specifics of this discipline will be discussed in the next chapter. For now, however, it needs to be said that this was the loyalty that sustained Rosemary through the difficult years of college. Her parents had taught her that she had the privilege of remaining pure for the sake of Christ. And she never wanted to let Him down.

These loyalties were entrenched in a little girl's heart by parents who talked about them. But they did much more than talk. Rosemary's parents lived these loyalties each day for her to see. Many parents today are scared that their children will succumb to peer pressures, and yet the parents themselves live a life of responding to peers. A child who sees his parents choose a twelve-thousand-dollar gold watch rather than a reasonably priced watch that tells time just as effectively will grow up lacking a role model in this area. Why does anyone want such a watch, except to impress his peers? Parents must realize that they are setting an example in everything they do. Children need to see that Mom and Dad have a higher accountability than to the family next door.

Loyalty and example must be coupled with one other factor: communication. Parents must be willing to talk to their children, and perhaps more significantly, parents must be willing to listen. Open parental ears that are not quick to judge will make it possible for young people to talk freely to the people who love them most.

Practicing to Handle Peer Pressure

Bobby's dad was well aware that Bobby was having a hard time dealing with the other boys in his tenth-grade class. This dad's first thought was to sit his son down and tell him that he knew there was a problem and then tell his son how to handle it. This was a wise dad, however. He knew that his lecture, no matter how loving, would only alienate Bobby.

They had just moved to the East Coast from Indiana, and Bobby was working at making new friends. He felt like an alien in a strange land. Dad was Bobby's only friend. To give him a lecture would only close out their line of communication, and make Bobby more lonely.

Bobby's dad chose to listen instead. "Let's go get a soda, Bobby," he suggested. While sitting in the booth drinking the soda, he asked about how things were going at school. "Oh, okay I guess," Bobby answered. "It's just not like back home."

"What's not like home," his dad asked, "the work or the kids?"

"The school work is about the same," Bobby answered. "It's the kids here. They're so cliquey. It's going to be hard to break in and make friends. They do things here that we never thought of, and they think it's cool."

As they continued talking, it became apparent that Bobby was afraid of how he would respond to the drugs and drinking that "all" the kids in his class seemed to be interested in.

"Are you afraid of whether you'll be able to resist or not, Son?" this Dad asked gently.

"No, that's not it, Dad," Bobby answered. "Actually I'm not sure I will know what to say when the time comes. I just don't want to come out sounding like a country bumpkin when I say no."

To this Bobby's dad responded with an idea. "Well, let's practice what you want to say."

"What do you mean, Dad?" Bobby asked.

"I mean let's make believe that I'm a kid asking you to do some of these things you don't want to do, and you practice what you want to say," this dad suggested. Before Bobby could object, his dad was on his feet walking away from the booth in this fast-food restaurant. He turned around, then came sauntering back in, trying to walk like a cool teen-ager. He asked Bobby if he wanted to go drink some beer. They both died laughing, but they also continued for quite a while until Bobby was able to help his dad create situations that were more lifelike. "What are you afraid of, Bobby?" his dad said, as he continued role playing situations such as dares from other boys. "There's nothing wrong with a beer—or don't they have beer yet out in Indiana?"

Together this father and son worked on the right words to use when dealing with peer pressure. The result was not only a night that brought them closer, but also a learning experience that Bobby was able to put into practice in the not-too-distant future.

It's easy for us to tell our children to "Just say no." But we must go further than that. It's up to parents to help them find and formulate the right words. And it's up to parents to help them practice, and have fun while practicing.

Peer pressure can never be avoided. Many parents, however, just give up altogether and throw their children to the wolves—or, should we say, the peers? Children must grow up knowing that they are part of an understanding family, a family that stands for something and has a past. They must see that theirs is a family that is worth being part of and loyal to. Even if this generation is the first to become Christian, the feeling of family loyalty can be started and nurtured.

Children must also grow up with an eye on the future. When they are making a decision to go with their peers, they must be taught to stack up that decision against their future. Would this betray my future spouse? Am I being loyal to my future spouse?

Children must also be helped to see that they were created by a God who loves them and has a special plan for their lives. Are their peers encouraging them to do something that would be disloyal to God?

Young people also need more than little pat phrases when dealing with peer pressure. Parents can help them prepare for what their peers will want them to do sexually, as well as in other areas, by giving their children the opportunity to practice the responses they really want to make.

And remember this: Nothing pushes a child into the grips of peer pressure more than a parent who is not willing to take the time to keep the parent-child relationship going. Parents who keep the lines of communication open and primed will help their children resist peer pressure. Parents who pass quick judgments without really listening, or who act shocked at what they hear, will push their children toward peer influence. Parents who listen and risk trusting their children will help the young person know that he is not alone in the battle.

Rosemary always felt that her parents were on her side and that they trusted her. She did not want to lose that trust. The efforts of Rosemary's parents gave her the personal discipline to deal with peer pressure and still be popular on a college campus. As her husband, I'm very grateful that they took the time to develop this maturity. I am reaping the benefits of their hard work.

Summary

1. Peer pressure can affect a person's moral code and spending habits.

2. Parents need to allow children to make purchases using their own money. This is especially true when they want items in response to social pressure.

3. Parents need to keep the lines of communication open and overtly show love to their children. If a child feels his parents are still on his team, it will make it easier for him to resist social pressures that encourage him to violate his own moral code.

24

The Discipline of Following a Philosophy of Life

YOU MAY HAVE HEARD the story of the little boy who refused to sit down at the table after being instructed to do so several times by his father. Each time the six-year-old just stood there defiantly. Finally the father got up and walked around the table to his young son. Placing his hands on the boy's shoulders, the father physically put his son in the chair. The boy looked up at his father and said, "I'm sitting on the outside, but I'm still standing on the inside."

That kind of response is certainly an important consideration in the parenting plan for discipline. We might be able to create changes on the outside, but it is what happens on the inside that will have a lasting effect on a child's behavior and life. The real question for every parent to respond to is, "How can I help my child mature on the inside?"

We all want to know how we can help our children develop a personal discipline that is firmly embedded on the inside. That way they will become self-disciplined and can respond to life's decisions appropriately, regardless of what is going on around them.

"How can I help my child internalize a consistent way of responding to the temptations of life?" one father asked. "How can I prepare him to respond to outside influences that he will encounter in the future? How can a parent help his child be self-disciplined for times when the parent is no longer available to help?"

The key to this training is instilling a firm philosophy of life. Self-discipline and maturity will not take place without it. This philosophy allows a child or an adult to see the bigger picture, rather than succumb to the here-and-now or live-for-the-moment attitude.

We all have our own personal philosophy, that significant thing we believe in and are counting on to get us through life. We discipline ourselves—or don't discipline ourselves—according to this philosophy which we believe will ultimately bring us happiness. Every parent teaches his or her child a philosophy of life by the example he sets. Our philosophy of life is the measuring stick we use to make decisions.

What is the basic thing we believe in? Some families seem to believe in little more than getting to the weekend. The parents might say that they have a deeper philosophy of life than simply living for the weekend and two days away from work. Yet the children watching them only see them pining away for a weekend at the lake. Or perhaps it's a savings account or pension that they see their parents counting on. Or it might even be education and the money it will eventually allow them to earn that is the philosophy parents are exemplifying to their children. Perhaps it is a more laid-back attitude of "live for today and shed the shackles of this world." If a parent believes capitalism and materialism are life's most important goals, that is what he teaches very plainly to the children.

Whatever option a parent chooses in this very important discipline we call philosophy of life, it will not only govern his own inner discipline, but it will ultimately influence the child's personal discipline for making life's decisions.

A system of discipline where the philosophy of life is not centered on God creates a relativistic approach to decision making. That kind of approach means a person's decisions will vary according to the situations and who is watching. For example, a relativistic philosophy of life espouses that it is sometimes beneficial to lie, while at other times it is not.

On the other hand, a system centered on God is consistent, the same regardless of the situation. It is rather obvious to me that a plan for helping the child learn personal discipline must include a relationship with the One who made us, who loves us, and who has already written a behavioral "blueprint" exemplified in the life of Christ. I am convinced that a plan built around faith in Christ will give the child the ultimate resource he needs in the quest for self-discipline.

It seems amazingly arrogant to me when parents act as if they can teach a child about the decisions of life without teaching them about the One who made life. That's like trying to maintain a Chevy by using a Maytag owner's manual. It just doesn't work. A family that demonstrates and teaches a faith in Christ as its philosophy of life helps the child see that there is a consistent basis for the decisions being made, and it also encourages the child to search the Bible for answers to his own questions.

Parents will not be able to anticipate every decision and temptation their children will face; thus they cannot prepare them with a specific response for every situation in life. But parents can help build within their children a philosophy of life that will help them respond consistently to whatever challenges to their character the future may bring.

Teaching by Example

As I've already pointed out, children learn their philosophy of life by what they see practiced in the family setting. In other words, teaching this element of self-discipline starts by providing good examples. If a parent wants a child to grow in a knowledge of Christ he or she must do much more than take the family to church. Far too many parents believe that this special lesson is the job of the church and its youth workers. Those are the same parents who are surprised when their children grow up attending church but have no personal understanding of Christianity. Parents who leave the Christian education to the youth workers lead the children to believe that Christianity is just for youth. That indicates that as one grows up he can leave the Christian stuff behind.

Children must grow up in a home where they see that faith in Christ is actually lived out in their parents' daily lives. For example, children should be able to see their parents participate in a personal time of devotions and Bible study each day. They should know that their parents pray about decisions they are making. Setting this kind of example shows the children that this philosophy of life is not something just for kids. It is something that the parents actually live by.

Many parents today say they do not want to influence their children in one religious direction or another. These parents feel that they would rather not teach a religious philosophy of life so as to let the children grow up and choose for themselves. Parents who do this are the ones who are shocked when their children become teen-agers and adults with no standard by which to make their decisions. Left without a consistent philosophy of life, children can do little more than accept the all-too-prominent philosophy that says, "live for today, but don't get caught." When these children do get caught, the parents don't know what went wrong.

Teaching a faith in something that will help children with their inner commitments and outer decisions will give those children a personal direction in life. It will give them that inner discipline we all desire for our children. But children must see their parents walking a philosophy of life that says Christ is preeminent in their lives and decisions—a life, for example, that says, "Son, I am faithful to your mom and I will always be faithful to her not just because I love her, though I do, but because I have a personal commitment to Christ. My philosophy of life is a personal inner discipline that calls me to obedience."

Teaching by Exposure

After setting an example, the second step in teaching a Christ-centered philosophy of life is consistent exposure to God's Word. Children need the opportunity to develop their faith by participating in family devotions. These are times of growing together as a family, while reading from a children's Bible or a children's devotional guide. Many families maintain this discipline of daily family devotions as they eat breakfast together. Others prefer spending time together in the evenings. Obviously, the simple fact that this time of reading the Bible together is done each day makes it a discipline in and of itself. There are many good books available that can help a parent begin this discipline of family devotions.

This routine will also expose the child to another discipline, that of developing a time of personal Bible reading and prayer. The child who is taught the importance of spending time each night reading the Bible and praying before bed will be given a very valuable opportunity to develop a relationship with the One who has the answers in life. This time spent each day is a discipline that will take awhile to develop; it cannot be just handed to our children. Learning the discipline of spending time with God happens only after a long period of practice.

When I was starting my doctoral studies, the university I was attending required me to take a library course. I thought it was a total waste of time. They wanted to teach me how to properly use the resources and research contained in that six-story building. By the time I had finished going through the drudgery of that course, I was amazed at all the materials that were available to me. I couldn't believe how easy it was to find the information that I needed for my own research. The parallel is obvious. There is so much available in a disciplined relationship with Christ. The child and young person just need to be taught how to find it. So often young people who are not exposed to this knowledge only spiral deeper into confusion as they take their lead from television shows. Others, however, have been given the key. Their parents have helped them develop the discipline of finding answers to life's decisions based on their relationship with God and a knowledge of His Word.

Experience—Using One's Philosophy of Life

The final step in the development of discipline in spiritual commitment is to allow the child to *use* and experience his philosophy of life. When children and young people come to the parent with requests, the wise parent will help them find the answers through their faith.

"Let's look at what you're asking to do," a father could say. "What does the Bible have to say?"

"That means no, doesn't it, Dad," the young person will probably respond.

"No, Son. That means that we need to learn to find answers from the wisdom of God rather than from my feeble efforts. That way we will always be consistent in the way we make decisions."

"But, Dad," this son pleads, "the Bible was written for a time long ago. This is two thousand years later. How can it help me with a decision about whether to go to the party or not? There probably weren't any parties back then."

Opportunities like this will help a young person see the relevance of the Bible as a tool for making decisions of self-discipline. The fourteen-year-old child may not run to his room ecstatically reaching for his Bible. But the effort will teach him how to do it for future reference. I wasn't dying to take that library course, but it proved invaluable when, at a later date I needed to know how to find information.

Children must be taught at an early age the discipline of learning to use the Bible as a resource manual for life. When my children come to me asking how to spell words, I do the same thing my father did. I send them to the dictionary so they will get comfortable using it. Likewise, with day-to-day questions, I point the children to the Lord and His Bible for the same reason.

This Christ-centered philosophy of life means that we discipline ourselves and our children to respond to the direction of God's leading, even when we don't understand. That is the discipline of faith. Many times I want my children to obey, even when they don't understand why I'm asking them to do something. I want them to have faith in my leadership. The same is true when responding to God's principles. It's not as important that we understand. It is more important that we trust.

Larry was a fourteen-year-old boy who came to live at Sheridan House because he had been having significant problems with his parents. Among other things, Larry had been extremely disrespectful and refused to respond to their authority. After living at Sheridan House for several months, Larry made a decision to follow Christ. This meant that he was choosing to make his philosophy of life one of obedience to Christ and the Bible. That decision was almost immediately tested. Larry had never been baptized and asked his counselor at Sheridan House if he could be baptized. The counselor told Larry to get his parents' permission.

"Why?" asked Larry, with his old defiance showing. "They're not even Christians, so why should I follow their rules in this matter?" The counselor responded by showing Larry that the Bible requires us to honor our parents and that it doesn't say to only honor our Christian parents.

When Larry asked his parents, the real test began. He returned after his weekend at home and announced, "I knew it was a bad idea to ask them. They only got mad and told me that I couldn't be baptized." Then Larry went on to confidently announce to his counselor that he wanted to be baptized anyway. Larry was shocked when the counselor told him that if he were baptized, it would be in contradiction to his new philosophy of life.

"What do you mean?" Larry asked. "Doesn't it say in the Bible that I should be baptized?"

"It does say that, Larry," the counselor explained. "But it also says that you should honor your parents. It doesn't say exactly when you should be baptized, but it does say to honor your parents. My suggestion is for you to wait until your parents give you permission. God must have a reason for postponing your baptism. You'll miss finding that reason if you don't stay consistent to your new philosophy of life and trust God on this one."

"That will never happen," Larry said sadly. "They'll never give me permission."

The counselor went on to explain to Larry that it was his job to show his parents that his new conversion was real—so real that they should let him be baptized. "Larry, this may take a very long time," the counselor said. "But one thing is for sure. They will never believe anything has changed in your life if you continue to fight them."

As it turned out, three months later Larry led both his parents to Christ, and they were all baptized together.

It is important to let the children experience the decisions that their new philosophy of life will bring. It is the parents' job to guide, set the necessary boundaries, and point their children toward the source book of that philosophy of life.

All of Rosemary's life, her parents led the family in devotions each morning. Her parents did everything they could to make this Bible reading exciting; but the children usually saw this ten-minute time as drudgery. Rosemary's parents were planting the precepts of God in the heart of their little girl, though. As she grew to become a teen-ager, she learned how to make decisions by watching their Godly example, by the exposure they gave her to God's Word, and through the opportunity they provided of experiencing a relationship with Christ. This philosophy of life helped her deal with life's confusions. When she was away from the guidance of her parents, she still maintained a disciplined, moral lifestyle. It was not the guidelines of her parents she was responding to then. She was able to remain pure because of the inner discipline she had learned as a result of her commitment to Christ.

Summary

Many young people today make undisciplined decisions because they are sent out into the world without a solid philosophy of life. Children must be taught, at an early age, that they were created in God's image and that He has a plan for them. Children need a philosophy of life to help them develop an inner discipline that will guide them in decisions when no one is around to help. To develop this inner discipline a parent can:

1. *Teach by example.* Set an example of what it means to follow Christ. Children must see that their parents believe this faith is so significant that Mom and Dad spend time each day that is devoted solely to God.

2. *Teach by exposure.* Children must be given exposure to this consistent philosophy of life by participating in daily family Bible readings and times of prayer.

3. *Teach by experience.* Children need opportunities of experiencing these disciplines on their own. They need instruction in how to develop and maintain a personal time with God. These are difficult disciplines to instill in the life of the child. They will have a more profound, life-long impact, however, than proper eating habits and other disciplines parents spend time on. It will affect what they do with their lives and bodies when we are not there to help.

PART VII

Perseverance: Disciplining Children in Difficult Situations

25

Discipline and the Single Parent

"WHAT ABOUT THOSE of us who are single parents? We barely have the time and energy to see that the kids brush their teeth, let alone deal with discipline. My children are out of control. How do I implement a plan for discipline?"

This is a standard question asked by single parents at parenting seminars. I discussed discipline and family life in the single-parent home in my first book, *Single Parenting: A Wilderness Journey*. The following chapter is written in response to single parents who read that book and want extra input about their particular needs pertaining to discipline. For simplicity's sake, the custodial parent will be referred to in the female gender, both to avoid having to constantly say "he or she," and because at the time of this writing, females make up 89 percent of the single-parent population.

There is probably no greater area of difficulty, as far as family configurations are concerned, as that of the single-parent home. Typical areas of concern are presented here in the form of questions from parents.

"How can I possibly do all the things stated in this book? I'm already exhausted just trying to get the family into bed every night. To tell you the truth, so far this book has only made me feel guilty about what I am not doing."

No parent will be able to instantly implement all the disciplinary plans laid out in this book. This book presents an ideal plan for each of us to attempt. If we, as parents, have no goals, then chances are we will reach no goals with our children. The single parent's first goal should be to attempt to get organized and stop living a life of simply responding to the dilemmas. Decide to stop being a crisis manager, bouncing from one catastrophe to the next. Make a decision to choose one area of discipline described in this book and then begin to implement it. Get a day-at-a-glance calendar and decide what time of what day this disciplinary area actually will be implemented. Remember, only take on one area of discipline at a time. Maybe establishing daily and weekly chores would be a good place to start.

"I have tried to give my children chores to do, and it's such a hassle that it's not worth it. Why shouldn't I just do it myself since I can do it faster and better?"

I question whether a parent can do chores faster once the child knows how to do the job. Two or three pairs of hands have to be better than one. But that isn't the real reason to give the children chores. They need to have responsibilities around the house for many reasons. One reason is that when they are older, their boss certainly will not see their ineptitude and kindly decide to do the job for them. We must teach our children how to work so that they will be prepared for the working world when they grow up.

Another reason for chores is that children need to feel that they are helping. Parents who fly around the room doing all the work, leaving their children sitting idle, make the children feel useless. When children feel that they are incapable of contributing, they don't feel like a valuable part of the family. And with this lowered sense of self-esteem, they are more prone to argue and fight with everyone around them. On the other hand, a child with a good feeling about himself will be less prone toward getting attention by being a negative force in the family.

Children must be given responsibilities, even if it does take extra work to teach them how to do it right. These responsibilities are a basic part of the disciplinary plan, as well as being good for the family self-esteem.

"My children and I argue about everything. As I read this book, I realized that the arguing was my fault. I can see that I am not at all consistent in my handling of discipline. But how can I start to be consistent at this late date?"

It is never too late to become consistent in a disciplinary plan. First, analyze a few of the areas that are causing the difficulty. Many times single parents are not consistent in the way they handle the children because the parent is operating from an emotion of guilt. The fact that the children have only one parent may not be the fault of the custodial parent. That is often irrelevant, however. The parent cannot help the fact that she feels sorry for the children. *Perhaps if I had done something differently, my children would have two parents at home,* some single parents think. That is not only wasted emotion, but it is also detrimental to the parenting plan. It causes emotions to dictate rather than the plan.

The emotion of guilt often causes the single parent to let the children talk them out of consequences or to do things like give the children too much money to spend. Whatever the guilty response, it only shows the children that it is not a plan that they are operating under. The house is operating under a parent who just gives in because she feels guilty.

Get rid of the feeling of guilt or anger when dealing with the children. Establish a plan and live with it. Sometimes single parents find it easier if they can find a friend to have coffee with once a week and discuss the disciplinary decisions being made at home. It is always good to have a friend or church support group to help us stay consistent.

Another reason for a lack of consistency is often just plain exhaustion. There it is, 6:00 P.M. and the single parent has just arrived home after retrieving the children from day care. Now it is time to do too many things. The children must be settled, homework must be started, and dinner needs to be prepared. Meanwhile the children will be attempting to get attention and their behavior will show it. Older children know that this is the perfect time to ask for permission to do things because, as one child told me, "Mom's too busy and tired to argue when she's getting dinner ready." In the exhaustion of the moment, the single parent often threatens, scolds—and then just gives in.

Priorities need to be established. What must the parent do first, rather than run around like a crazy person trying to do everything at once? Ten minutes could be set aside to sit and talk to the children. Then the parent could start with, "Whose day is it to help me get dinner ready?" The key here is to get regimented. Try to do it the same way every night. That way the children know what comes next, and they have the security of living in a system with boundaries.

"Isn't this really a waste of my time since the children spend every weekend with my Ex? His lifestyle is totally different from mine. Doesn't he completely undo everything I am trying to do?"

Reestablishing Order

Many single parents face a real dilemma at the end of every weekend when the children are returned home in one of two ways. Some children are dropped off completely out of control because they have spent the weekend in a system with no boundaries. Others come home loaded with toys and other goodies after being showered all weekend with gifts. First, let's deal with the mom who may dread the Sunday-night scenario of trying to calm the children who've just returned from an out-of-control weekend. While she sorts their dirty clothes, she must listen to them talk about the things they did or saw that she would never permit to happen in her house.

The first rule of dealing with visitation heartaches is not to pump the children for information about their weekend with their dad. Do not use them to spy on their own father.

The second significant factor in single parenting, or all parenting for that matter, is not to try to control what you cannot control. Most single parents will not be able to change the situation that the children go into when they are on visitation. To attempt to change the fact that their dad never gets them to bed on time or that he constantly allows them to eat things they should not be eating will only cause tremendous frustration. The fact that two ex-spouses could not communicate when they were married is certainly not going to change or improve after the divorce. It is rare when ex-spouses can advise each other on parenting skills.

There are many more serious and heartbreaking situations that the children may go into when they are away for visitation. The children may encounter drugs or a live-in girlfriend at Dad's house. If nothing can be done legally to change the situation, and unfortunately that is most often the case, then work hard not to ridicule the child's dad. Yes, a statement may need to be made such as, "I know that is happening, Johnny, and it makes me very sad. We need to pray that God will help your daddy see that it is wrong to live with someone before being married." And be aware that even a comment like that can come back to haunt the single mom. When Johnny lets Dad know that the family is praying for him because he is sinning, most dads will not respond kindly. Even though that may be the case, some comment should be made to help Johnny understand this is not acceptable behavior.

Is it a waste of time to try so hard when the other parent's behavior and attitude seems to be so contradictory? Actually the opposite is true; that's when such efforts are most badly needed. A child who spends time living in two contrasting environments will eventually learn that one system operates on love and a consistent plan, while the noncustodial parent's system may operate on bitterness and an anything-goes attitude. Though the weekend system with no plan of action may sometimes seem like fun to the child, it is actually a very insecure setting. One child told me, "It's fun at Dad's because I can stay up as late as I want to.

But I never know where I stand. Sometimes I can do something that is wrong, and he doesn't say anything at all. Other times I do the same thing, and he threatens to take me home early. I always feel like I'm walking on eggshells at Dad's. To tell you the truth, I am always relieved to get home. At least with Mom I always know where I stand."

When the children come home from a wild visitation, the single parent should sit them down and give them a minute to adjust to the old system at home. They may have a real need to talk about the weekend. Once again, do not probe for information. When they have had a turn to talk, then help them return mentally to the structure of the home by going over the plan for the remainder of the night. "Children, it is now 8:30. You know that you have thirty minutes to get your bath, brush your teeth, and get in bed. If you are done with all that before 9:00, then as usual, I will read you a story. Now here is your snack and then you can head on to the bath. Whether or not we have a story tonight is your choice."

Quickly put them back into a system and put the responsibility on their shoulders. You can only work with what is under your roof; that is all God will hold you accountable for.

In the second scenario, when children return from visitation bearing toys and good-time tales as if they have just come back from Disneyland, your first thought may be that the noncustodial parent is behind on child support, but he sure buys a lot of toys for the children when he has them for the weekend. Don't get into the game of competing with this attempt to buy love. Discipline yourself not to feel inadequate when he buys all the fun things and you can't because you're hardly able to buy groceries. The children need to learn financial discipline from at least one parent. Do not let guilt and anger put you into a position of financial irresponsibility. Don't buy those things you can't afford.

Nor should a parent respond to games such as, "Dad lets us stay up as late as we want." Avoid voicing anger and judgment when responding to these statements: "Children, you know that this is the way we do it here. Hurry and finish so that I can read you a story."

These anecdotes are not meant to imply that all the noncustodial parents are irresponsible. That is certainly not the case. In many situations it is the custodial parent who is providing the child with the worst parental example and disciplinary plan. In those cases the noncustodial parent must take advantage of the times of visitation to provide an environment of consistent boundaries and a lot of love. The noncustodial parent should fight the temptation to want to primarily be a friend to the child. The first job is to be a parent and that means supplying leadership. Use the weekend to teach the child about living in an environment that has family responsibilities. This parent must dramatically exhibit the ethnic qualities of the Italian and the German families described earlier in this book. Use the weekend to train the child rather than to entertain the child. When possible the noncustodial parent should make contact with the custodial parent to find out what routine the child is used to. The child will benefit greatly from a system that is as similar as possible to the other home he lives in.

"Why do my children seem to push the boundaries so hard when I desperately need their cooperation?"

Children push to find walls or rules. If a child senses that his environment is out of control, it is natural for him to push against it in order to signal the parent in charge, "Hey, isn't anybody going to get charge of this situation?" Children are much happier in an environment that has consistent rules. When the consistency doesn't exist, it is almost as if the children exhibit behavior that will force a parent to take charge.

One single parent who participated in one of our seminars wrote me a letter that illustrates this. After the seminar she returned home and announced to her daughter that she was sorry there had been no system. "From now on," she said, "I want us both to try harder to live within the boundaries of this new plan." The mother went on to explain the system, and the daughter just sat there with a very sullen look on her face. This was a girl who had been very rebellious.

At the end of the first week several skirmishes had been fought. The mother had been successful in her effort to be calm and consistent, but she was exhausted by Saturday. She decided to reward herself by having her hair done. When she returned home with her new hairstyle, her daughter sat down next to the mother on the couch. Then the daughter said a very interesting thing. "We're going to make it, Mom, aren't we?" she asked confidently.

This mother was shocked by that statement. As they talked, it became apparent that the daughter had lived with the fear that her whole world was going to cave in because their home had been so chaotic and without leadership. The girl felt that since Mom finally felt confident with a plan of action and now was taking care of herself by having her hair done, this was a sign they were "going to make it." In a perverse way this girl had subconsciously been pushing and fighting her mother in order to force Mom to get control and become strong. The children in the single-parent home desperately need to see that Mom knows what she is doing. Their behavior often screams for leadership.

There is no easy way for single parents to implement a parenting plan. I know from personal experience that it can be done, however. I am the product of a single-parent home. The area of greatest encouragement for me was the fact that my dad knew nothing about parenting when he suddenly found himself alone after my mother's death. He worked at establishing a very consistent disciplinary plan for his children, and then he, himself, set the example. He lived a disciplined, moral life, staying within his own boundaries. That way we learned by his example. I am grateful today for his personal discipline. His children often fought him, but he never gave up. He is an example to me of what single parents can do if they make parenting the priority in their lives.

Summary

1. Single parents should attempt to implement a disciplinary plan in their home one step at a time. Don't try to change the whole household environment in one weekend, month, or even year. Take one behavior at a time and establish a plan to deal with it.

2. It's never too late to begin establishing a plan to help your child. The key is to begin.

3. The single parent cannot be responsible for what the child does or is permitted to do when he is visiting his noncustodial parent. Don't use the inconsistencies from home to home as an excuse. Do what you can do in your home.

26

Discipline in the Blended Family

SUSIE AND BILL dated for two years. Both had previously been married and then divorced. After this period of dating, they got married, bringing two children each into a new family configuration. "The Brady Bunch," a television series, had made it look so easy. Susie and Bill couldn't figure out why discipline quickly became so difficult after they were married.

While doing research for my dissertation on single parenting, I came across several studies that revealed some interesting findings concerning behavior in the blended family. The results of the research indicated that blended families had more disciplinary problems than any other family configuration, even more than single-parent homes. Blending two families is not an easy task. Susie and Bill were finding out that the children were responding to them differently now that they were married, and they couldn't figure out what was happening.

Life Before the Blend

All the roles change when the wedding takes place. Prior to the wedding the single parent and child have a very special relationship. Often Mom's bed is a fun place for parent and child to spend time talking together. Single parents and their children may even watch television together and sleep all night in that master bed.

The oldest child in the family generally holds a very special position in the single-parent home. The parent may confide in the oldest child and develop a friendship relationship as well as a parent-child relationship. In fact, this may have caused some disciplinary problems when the child was in the friendship mode with his mom and she was responding to him as his parent.

Many of these things change after the wedding, including the master bedroom. The door is closed for the first time in years, and the double bed that was a place for the family to congregate is now off-limits. No longer can the child feel comfortable in bed with his parent. Perhaps he is not even permitted in there anymore.

The oldest child might have to deal with the fact that his position as partner to the single parent has been usurped. By one brief ceremony, the child is returned to the station of child. This loss of power, and possibly even a feeling of losing an intimate relationship, is enough to cause bitterness. "It made me mad that my mom could be so happy with someone other than me," a child said. This statement by Susie's fifteen-year-old was evidence that Susie had allowed herself to become too dependent on the friendship of her oldest child. Now she was paying a price for leaning on this boy. He was bitter and felt displaced rather than happy for his mom.

Another area of confusion often takes place before the marriage. During the dating time the adults sometimes don't know what to have the children call their fiancé. In an effort to help create a relationship between fiancé and child, a mistake is often made. The child may be encouraged to call the other adult by his or her first name. Instead of calling him Mr. Smith as he did for months, all of a sudden the child is encouraged to call him Fred or Uncle Fred. This might be the only adult in the child's life that he calls by a first name. Then the wedding takes place, and many children face the same problem adults face with their parents-in-law when they get married. Now what do I call this older person?

It is fine and healthy for the children to continue to use the prefix "Mr." right up until the marriage. Anything else not only causes confusion but brings the adult's position down to one of a peer rather than a parental position after the marriage has taken place. Some people have even gone so far as to allow the children to call the fiancé Mom or Dad while they are dating. This is a very dangerous move for the child. The expectations and the possibility that a wedding might not take place could only lead the child into another loss. Referring to the other adult as Mr. Smith is safest and makes the most sense because it's the title that the child uses with his teachers and every other adult outside his family.

Children need to be prepared for the wedding only after the couple is confident one is actually going to take place. At that point a parent would be wise to let the children play very significant parts in the preparation and ceremony itself. Children need to feel included, rather than like excess baggage.

After the Wedding

After the wedding a meeting should occur to answer children's doubts about several things. "I always wondered whether my new mom married just my dad or the whole family. Did she really want us, or did we just come along with the package?" one child said. This is a natural question on the hearts of many children.

In the meeting, the children must be assured that they are a wanted part of this new union. They also need help to decide what to call their new parent. In my own life, when my dad got remarried, I went for years wondering what to call this lady who had married my dad. When they were dating, I called her by her first name. After the wedding it seemed to be inappropriate. I basically decided that when I talked to her I would not use a title. I remember the struggle of sitting at the dining-room table, waiting for her to make eye contact with me so I could ask her to pass the potatoes without having to get her attention by using a name or title. I just had no idea what to call her. Finally, sensing my difficulty, she decided to help me out.

A meeting was called one night at the kitchen table. "I want to talk to you about something," she began. "I can sense that you don't know what to call me when you are talking to me." I remember feeling stupid at being caught, and so I defended myself by denying it was a problem. "Well, anyway," she went on, "I know that I am not your biological mother, and I also know that I could never begin to take her place. I don't want you to think that I would ever try to do that. I am, however, the mother of this house. What I mean is, I fill the position of mother here. It would make me very proud if you would call me Mom just because that's my role here. You certainly don't have to do that. It's up to you. I just want you to know that I would be happy for you to do that."

With that talk she accomplished a lot. She established her position of authority as the mother of the house. She also gave us the proper name to call her rather than using her first name. My younger brother began calling her Mom immediately. It was okay to do now that he had been given permission. It took me a long time to follow his lead, but she never knew how good it made me feel to know she would allow us to consider her our mom. She solved a multitude of problems with that talk, not the least of which was the fact that she gently let us know that she did not consider herself our friend. She was going to be an authority figure in the home.

Becoming a family takes time. It doesn't just happen with a ceremony. Many staff meetings need to be held to clear the air of misunderstandings. It will take time for the children to feel safe and accepted by the new person in the home. The status of parent is something that is earned over time. Many step-parents try too hard. They want to be accepted so much that they try to be a friend. That only puts them in a difficult position when disciplinary measures must be taken.

Step-parents should go very slowly in this fragile setting. They should be careful not to invade the personal space of each individual child because too much physical contact at first may be awkward or misinterpreted. A parenting relationship takes a long time to develop.

Once again the key is consistency in the disciplinary plan. Parents will have to make it a point to get together several times a week at first. These meetings should be used to discuss the children and work toward maintaining a plan. Honesty will be extremely important, as both parents will be very sensitive about their own children. For years each parent has had to care for the children alone. Now another adult is on the team. This is a time to blend ideas and compromise on ways to handle issues.

If parents are not able to talk and compromise, they will go into the difficult situation of being two families living in one home. Parents must be together in the way they deal with all the children. The parents must also be prepared for a child who may work very hard at breaking up their relationship. Many children dream about being a hero in the life of their parents, and the most heroic thing they could imagine would be to be the catalyst to bring their two divorced parents back together. The only way to do that is to attempt to break up the new marriage.

The couple in the blended home has a tremendous opportunity to show the children a marriage that is committed to stay together. The children need the opportunity of seeing a husband and wife who adore each other. That teaches them it can be done. Show the children a strong relationship that is consistent in its handling of the disciplinary plan, and understand it will take time and many staff meetings before there is open communication.

An especially difficult area of understanding for the child will be the new priority relationship in the family. Prior to the marriage the single mom protected her children—it was just mother and child against the world. The children learned that they were the priority of their mother's existence. Now that she is married, however, the priority relationship must change to focus on the marriage. Understandably, children will have a difficult time understanding this shift. Many will feel betrayed and alienated. Parents will have to work hard to show the child that the husband and wife are working to become one flesh in their relationship. One mother said she explained it like this, "Son, you have not lost me. Actually you have gained a more complete mom. Haven't you noticed that I am happier and less frustrated in the way I have been responding to you? It's because I am married now and your step-father and I are working at becoming one flesh. We are working at becoming so much in love that we will be better parents for you. You haven't lost your single mom. You've gained a more fulfilled parent."

One other thing must be said in this chapter on discipline in the blended family. One of the most disastrous mistakes that can be made by a step-parent is for him to make a negative comment about the children's natural father. That forces the children to take sides, and the step-parent will always find himself on the losing side in this situation. No matter what kind of person the natural father may be, he is still their father, and they came from him. The children will never be able to deal with negative comments about the person they dream about and call Dad. Stay away from situations that force the children to take sides. Everyone will lose.

It is very difficult for children to deal with a new parent figure in their life. They have dreamed of what it would be like, and no new parent will be able to meet these dreamland expectations. Only a consistent plan for discipline will show the child that the new parent is not out to hurt him. A consistent plan will make it possible for step-parent and child to finally become parent and child.

Summary

1. A child in the blended household endures many drastic changes. Before the marriage he may have had mom's full attention. Now that she's remarried, the child may feel abandoned.

2. Becoming a new family takes time.

3. Becoming a new family takes communication.

4. Becoming a new family takes permission.

5. Becoming a new family takes a willingness to compromise.

27

"But You Don't Know Where I Live!"

RECENTLY I WAS speaking in Southern California, and the parents were telling me that they thought it was next to impossible to raise a child there. They wanted to move to Northern California where they assumed the environment would be more conducive to families. I returned home to speak at a conference in Florida and heard similar comments from some of those parents. By the way some of the parents were talking, one would almost believe that God Himself had established a sanctuary in the mountains of North Carolina!

I had to laugh. These parents actually seemed to believe that they could do a better job of raising their children in North Carolina than they could in Florida. It was funny to me because I had grown up right outside New York City, certainly not a place they would have chosen to raise their families. I left New York to go to college in the Smoky Mountains of North Carolina. During my senior year of college there in the mountains, I did some work with high-school students from a nearby town. I was amazed at the teen drug use and the number of teen pregnancies that were occurring in this little mountain city. The problems in that mountain sanctuary were as bad as the problems I had seen in New York, or the problems I would see in South Florida. There was a difference, however. In New York and South Florida parents admitted their youth were having a problem, and they set up programs to deal with it. In this little mountain town in the Smokies parents denied that the high-school kids were having any problems at all. As a result, the young people were going without help.

No Place to Hide

There is no way to change locations and walk away from society's problems. Television has made our nation almost like one big city. Kids in Indiana know the same things about life as the young people in Philadelphia. If any location is in danger, perhaps it is those places where parents are lulled into believing that their children won't have to deal with temptation. These are the parents that believe it is still a Mark Twainian world where they can send their son, Huck, out the door and check on him ten hours later. That world doesn't exist anywhere.

A friend recently finished rearing three daughters to adulthood. The first two were growing up while the family lived in a city in the Bible Belt of the deep South. The youngest daughter, however, spent most of her life growing up in South Florida after the father got transferred. As my friend watched her youngest daughter finish college, she made a very interesting observation.

"My first two girls grew up in a very old, sleepy Bible Belt city, and we had thought it was the ideal place to raise a family. Everyone was so nice that we would let our girls go pretty much wherever they wanted to go. We assumed that everyone was just like us primarily because everyone was going to church and appeared to have the same values. If one of the girls wanted to spend the night at a friend's house, it was no problem. Often we didn't even check. In fact, we didn't think it necessary to talk to these girls very much about life. Somehow we got lulled to sleep.

"We were horrified when the airlines transferred Jack to South Florida. After all, what kind of place could South Florida be to raise a family? As we moved, our two older daughters were going out the door, each to a Christian college," she recalled.

"Everything has happened just the opposite as we expected. The daughter we raised in South Florida is doing wonderful things with her life. I guess that's because we assumed nothing when raising her. We spent a lot of time talking to her and helping her understand what the temptations of the world were like. She had no illusions about our neighbors, many of whom did not go to church. My youngest saw that it was generally only the ones who believed as we did who went on Sundays. That definitely had not been the case where we used to live.

"My youngest had the opportunity to see a lot of confusing things and because we were more conscious of our parenting responsibilities, we were available to listen and be there to help. She could make mistakes while she was still home, and we could help her work through them. Her older sisters have had a much more difficult time, however. As parents, we were lulled to sleep where their training was concerned. We thought they were in a protected environment. Now, as we hear them talk and watch them handle their social life, we realize we were wrong.

"As it turns out, the daughter we raised in South Florida is much more confident in who she is. She is at a secular university today and is much stronger about what she believes in than her sisters were at her age. I guess that is because her sisters didn't receive the parental input that she did. We didn't realize how much more we needed to be doing as parents when we raised the first two.

"It may sound funny, but today I am happy I raised my daughter in South Florida. It helped me do a good job, and it helped prepare my daughter for life in the real world."

That was not a statement about Christian colleges versus secular colleges. It was a comment made by a mother at the end of a seminar illustrating that parents should never find a comfortable confidence in their environment. We need to parent, no matter where we live. She could sense that many younger parents felt that they were in the wrong place to raise a family. This experienced mom very wisely wanted to help the other parents see that it doesn't matter where you live.

Lot raised his daughters in a despicable city called Sodom (Genesis 19). This city was so bad, everyone had to be off the streets before nightfall. It seems that the men were even attempting to rape two guests of Lot's. Sodom was so bad, God decided to wipe it off the face of the earth.

Lot was living in this disgusting place. Yet it appears that he was doing a good job of raising his family. It could be that he was so conscious of all that was going on around him that he was trying extra hard to be a good parent. At any rate, he was considered to be a righteous man. He and his family were such a contrast from the rest of the inhabitants of Sodom that they were given an opportunity to escape before its destruction.

Lot is a prime example of the fact that it doesn't matter where we live when raising our children. The thing that really matters is what we are doing with the children who have been temporarily put in our care. Many parents are waiting for that time when they will be wherever they think that ideal place is to raise a family. In the interim, they are neglecting to do the job assigned to them. We all should spend less time worrying about *where* we are raising our children and more time concerned with *how* we are raising them.

Children are on loan to us so that we can train them. It is a parent's job to help a child learn many things, not the least of which is personal discipline. It must and can be done no matter where a family lives. A couple of years ago I needed to borrow a friend's extra car for a week. I was very conscious of taking good care of the car because it belonged to someone else. It's funny how I drive the car I own very differently from a borrowed one. Sometimes I don't even wash my own car for weeks at a time, and yet I washed that borrowed car after only five days of use.

Often we treat children as though we own them, rather than as if they are only loaned to us. One day, as they go out the door, we will be returning them into the hands of their Owner. I believe we will be held accountable for the way we cared for this special responsibility.

Summary

1. It's not where you live that makes the difference with your children. It's what you do.

2. Parents cannot allow their environment to raise their children. We must assume that no matter where we live, our children will need our constant love and attention.

28

"But Mine Isn't Responding"

CATHY AND BILL had three children, all in their teens. Two of the children were model boys; but Allen, their youngest, had always been a child who marched to a different drum. Already, by his mid-teens, he had run away seventeen times. These parents were tremendously frustrated. "We have tried everything, and Allen just doesn't respond," Bill said, with great frustration.

I write this chapter with considerable hesitation. I do not want to leave any parents with an excuse not to do the job of parenting. There are many parents who believe nothing can be done with their unruly child. In reality the real problem is that nothing has ever been done. The child got to the point of being out of control because there was never a consistent plan in place. Each decade seems to have its own phrase or excuse for children who have not been taught to behave. The labels are legitimately applied to those children who don't respond to a plan in the same way as the majority of children do. Unfortunately many other parents give children these labels to soothe their own guilt for not doing the proper parenting job. One decade used the legitimate label of "hyperactive." There were and still are children who are really hyperactive or suffering from Attention Deficit Disorder with Hyperactivity. I sympathize with those parents who truly have a child with this difficult condition. We work with many such children at Sheridan House, and it is a very frustrating disorder for parent and child. Too many other parents, however, have mistakenly concluded that their own children have this disorder when, in fact, these parents simply have not established a plan and thus cannot control their children.

Accepting the Unexplainable

This chapter is for those parents like Cathy and Bill who have instituted a plan and consistently maintained it, but to no avail. Allen hasn't responded to anything. There are some steps that should be taken by parents like Cathy and Bill. It must be emphasized, however, that there are no easy answers.

The first thing a parent must do if the child is not responding is to sit down and check the disciplinary plan. Is the child responding out of frustration because the plan is not handled in a consistent manner? Perhaps the plan is consistent but too complicated or too long-term for the child to understand. For some children four days is too long to wait for a positive or negative response from a parent. For some children four hours is too long.

If at a parenting staff meeting it is decided that the plan has been consistently handled for quite a while and the child is still not responding, the next step is to look for a signal. Is the child's behavior defiant rather than forgetful? Forgetful means the plan spans too great a period of time. Defiant may mean the child is signaling something to the parent. Have there been any changes in the child's life or environment to cause him to be disturbed? Has the family recently moved? Has a pet died? Has a friend turned away? Is the child attending a new school or classroom, or are there any other changes that the parents can find that might affect the child? Defiant behavior may signal something has happened and the child simply does not have the words to describe his difficulty in dealing with the situation. He acts out as an expression of pain.

In the case of Cathy and Bill there was no such incident. In fact, the difficult behavior they were dealing with was not a result of entering puberty or any other discernible change. Allen had responded in this way to their authority since he could walk.

The next step for this couple was to ask their pediatrician for help. Perhaps there was an allergy or other physiological problem that Allen was dealing with and this affected his responses to life. In their case they were looking for a diet to help their son. Perhaps the doctor could prescribe some medication. After a long series of tests by several doctors, however, it was determined that there was no physiological explanation for Allen's behavior.

The pediatrician's suggestion was for this family to visit a family counselor, who began his work by administering his own series of tests. After months of work and counseling, Bill and Cathy were told what they had thought might be the case all along. With a few exceptions, these parents had done a wonderful job of parenting.

In our Western culture today we have developed a mentality that everything has an explanation and solution. One of the reasons many people find it irrational to respond to life by faith is because they have been indoctrinated to believe that the human race can figure out everything. This arrogance often causes many of us to fail to accept the inevitable. Some things are simply unexplainable, and we must accept them as they are. Bill and Cathy had not done anything wrong to cause Allen to respond to life with the rebellion that he was carrying. It was their role to accept him and yet continue to work with him.

A Commitment to Parenting

Several years ago I remember hearing a story on the national news that left me with a permanent impression of what commitment to parenting is all about. A boy in England was born paralyzed to the point where he could not move any of his limbs nor could he even chew properly. The boy's mom decided to accept this child as an opportunity for great parental sacrifice. She taught him to read as he was growing up, and yet he could not talk. This mom decided to teach her son how to write even though he had no use of his hands. By inventing a device that she strapped to his head, she taught him how to peck out one letter at a time on a typewriter. To add to the difficulty, she had to stand behind him the entire time and support his wobbling head as he worked at tapping the keys.

This boy finally got to the point that he could type about one page a day. That was done over an eight- to ten-hour period with the mom holding her son's head the entire time. She did it because she accepted what she had to deal with. She didn't spend any time searching for guilt or embracing pity. When neighbors and friends tried to discourage her, she ignored them. Finally she achieved success. No, it wasn't a prime-time television fairy tale where he got up and walked one day, and later ran for president. The boy simply learned to write while she laboriously encouraged him by holding his head for hours without rest. This story was a national news item because the boy wrote a best-selling book. When they attempted to interview the young author, he awkwardly typed out the words, "I owe it all to a mom who never gave up, no matter how much of a burden I became."

No, there aren't solutions and disciplinary plans that every child will respond to. The key is for the parents to go overboard in setting up a very easy-to-understand plan and then shower the child with love. He needs to see extremes. This child will typically be very lonely, as he may have very few friends. To add to the burden, the parent may be the only playmate this child has. He will need to feel forgiven and loved, no matter how far short he falls from perfection. Most children eventually grow through these behavioral problems. It will be significant for the parent to help him get through with the least amount of scars.

One other area is very important for the parents of the Allens of the world to understand. This child's behavior can exact a very heavy toll on the parents' marriage if they do not stay very close together. Typically, the mother will spend much of her time exhausted while the father will spend his time feeling inadequate. It will be significant for the parents to have many weekly staff meetings. It is also important that the child does not perceive himself as a burden to the relationship. One of the greatest things the parents can offer this child is a picture of marital and family commitment. The other is to lead the child to Christ at an early age and continue to disciple him. When he is grown, he too may say, "I owe it all to my parents who never gave up or got discouraged."

Summary

Parents who are dealing with a child that does not seem to be responding to their disciplinary plan can decide to take a step-by-step approach to help the child.

1. First, the parents should analyze their parenting plan. Is it consistently handled and arranged in a way that the child can understand?

2. If a consistent plan is not helping the child's behavior, the next step is to see if the child is attempting to give the parents a signal.

3. The parents of this child can turn to their pediatrician to look for physical causes behind the child's behavior.

4. A counselor's help can be sought to look for possible emotional or learning difficulties that may explain the child's behavior.

5. Many parents will not find solutions and will be put in a position of accepting the opportunity of simply having a great impact on their child. The child who is disruptive, even though his parents are doing everything in their power to help him, will owe much to his parents' love and perseverance. This can be seen as quite a privilege.

PART VIII

Conclusion: What It All Boils Down To

29

Pizza Crust

"I HATE THE CRUST, Dad," my son was saying one evening as the family was eating a pizza. "Why do they have to make pizza with a crust anyway?"

"Well, Robey," I began to explain, "if there wasn't any crust, it would be very hard to eat the part of the pizza that you like. The crust is the part that holds the whole thing together. Without the crust to support the bottom and give walls for the sauce, what do you think this pie would look like?" Robey responded understandingly by saying, "A soup."

This seemingly ridiculous Saturday-evening conversation all of a sudden took a very profound turn. My daughter, who had been listening, said, "The crust is kind of like the rules around the house, isn't it, Dad?" Not being real quick on my feet, but trying to sound like the family sage, I responded with, "What do you mean by that, Torrey?"

"I mean the rules hold the family together just like the crust holds the pizza sauce together. Without crust and rules we couldn't get to have the things we want like the good part of the pizza and fun at home."

Wow! Where did this kid get all that brilliance? Must be from her mom! Torrey was exactly right. Families won't be able to enjoy the good things of life if they don't first create a crust—a good disciplinary plan.

Everybody has a favorite unmarried brother or friend who loves to come over and visit the children. But the play quickly gets out of hand. Somehow he has developed a habit of coming over and before anybody knows what is happening, he is wrestling with the children on the living-room floor. It's a fun time, but unfortunately that is all he knows how to do with the children. This unmarried friend has no idea how to stop the children from jumping on him. He has established no boundaries with the children. When he says to the children, "Okay, kids, that's enough now," the kids know he doesn't really mean what he

186

says. Eventually either a parent has to rescue the well-intentioned man or he just stops coming over to visit, all because he doesn't know how to institute a plan of discipline. He has no "crust" in his relationship with the children so he can no longer enjoy the good parts.

Discipline Provides a Job Description

Crust certainly isn't the best part of the family relationship—but it is essential. Many parents love their children, but they find it difficult to like them. "I don't know what's wrong with our family," one dad said. "Maybe it's just me. We all spend half the year looking forward to vacation. It's the talk of the family as we plan all the fun things we are going to do. And then the day arrives, and almost from the moment we get in the car, it's a disaster. The kids fight and argue all the way to the cabin we rent. It doesn't get any better when we get there, either. They seem to argue with each other for the entire two weeks. I love my children, but I don't enjoy spending time with them. I can't wait to get back to the office. I just don't like them very much sometimes."

Vacations are a prime example of times when families are away from their crust. The rules, even if they exist at home are usually different when families are on vacation. Parents may not take the time to establish a daily routine, and so they are left with two options: either see that the children are entertained the whole time or live with the anarchy.

It's difficult for a child to exist in a role that has no job description. One of my first jobs out of college was like that. There was no set time to be at the office and everyone left whenever he or she wanted to. The work we were to do was handled in a similar way. I found myself being very paranoid, arriving earlier than everyone else and staying late. I spent my time looking over my shoulder, wondering if I was doing a good job. I had no way of knowing, since there was no job description. Very shortly I found that I was becoming irritated with my co-workers and their poor work habits. I kept wondering why the boss didn't do something, and I soon lost respect for his leadership. It is very difficult to work with no job description. Sometimes, especially in unusual situations like vacations, we ask children to exist in a setting with no job descriptions. Parents think that it will be a nice break for the children to be away from rules. The children, however, quickly signal the parents that they need the boundaries.

A plan of discipline allows the family to enjoy the more important things of life: spending time talking together, sharing family devotions, reading books, going out to restaurants. These activities can be a fun time for everyone in a family that has a disciplinary plan.

Families that are not consistent in their plan will spend their times together arguing. The family interaction will consist of one ongoing power struggle, with the big question being, "Who's in charge here?"

Discipline Enables Commitment

A parent who does not take the time or go to the effort to establish a consistent disciplinary plan in the home dooms the family to be a collection of individuals who never get along or learn how to cooperate. Many years ago a man came to Green Bay, Wisconsin, as the new coach of a team that was not considered to be much of a professional franchise. The late Vince Lombardi brought with him one very basic plan: *discipline*. Those rugged football players had never seen anything like it. He established the rules, presented them to the team, and they all but laughed at him. Then he consistently enforced every boundary that he had created. Slowly a miracle occurred. This once-undisciplined group of individuals became a team. Actually it became more than a team; it became a family that was also the greatest professional football team in the world at that time.

It happened because someone took charge in a fair way, with a plan that everyone could follow successfully. No longer was there a constant power struggle. Now this "family" was melded together and secure in the fact that the leader knew what he was doing. Many of those Green Bay Packers who played under Coach Lombardi are very successful in a wide variety of other professions today. When interviewed recently on television, it was amazing to hear each one of them praise his former football coach. One after another, each man said that Lombardi's personal example and disciplinary plan for life had helped him become the man he is today, long after football.

Lombardi's consistent discipline made it possible for these men to reach new heights of excellence. He helped them learn to get themselves under such close personal control that they really knew what the word *commitment* meant. Too often that character quality is missing in our society today. Perhaps we have heard too many commercials that say "have it your way." Would we but listen as our country, our families of the future, and the work of our Lord cry out for the next generation to commit themselves to the point of suffering. Without personal discipline there can be no sacrificial commitment.

Discipline Now Will Protect Tomorrow

Discipline in the home protects our children from the future, when they will face many situations and temptations requiring them to make decisions. A lack of personal discipline, the inability to walk away when "everyone else is doing it," could cause them to curse their lives forever. Children need to grow up in a home that emphasizes a personal discipline that will give them the inner strength to make good moral decisions. They must be strong enough to say "No. Though it may look good on the surface, it would curse my life." Children who grow up in homes that overindulge them will be too immature to understand that they cannot have everything that they want.

Discipline in the home will help a child reach his full potential. Few of life's goals come to us by an easy route. Children need to understand the discipline that it takes to endure. Mankind's greatest accomplishments have been done by adults who are able to keep working long after others have given up.

Discipline Helps Teach Forgiveness

Discipline in the home helps a family get along. As members of the home learn how to fit into the family unit, they also will be preparing themselves for the time when they must blend into other institutions, such as their job, their church, and their own future family. Cooperation will also allow the family to loosen up and have fun together. Such an environment will be healthy for the emotional development of the children and for their self-esteem.

A home that offers a good solid crust will provide children the opportunity to learn about Christ. It takes personal discipline to spend the necessary time to develop and learn about the Christian life. Children who live in constant struggle with the authority figures in their home will find it difficult to learn and trust their heavenly Father.

One very significant reason that children have trouble understanding how God could love them is the fact that they do not understand what it means to feel forgiven. The concept of forgiveness is extremely significant to the parent-child relationship, as well as to one's relationship with God. A child who does not feel forgiven lives in constant insecurity. "Do my parents really love me, or are they still mad at me for what I did today?" If there is no plan, then there is no way for a child to know if he has received a consequence for his unacceptable behavior. And if there has been no predetermined consequence, then chances are that the parents have responded to the child in a manner that exhibited frustration and anger. That will mean the child has no opportunity to know he is forgiven. Where there is no forgiveness, there is a very uneasy relationship.

Children need to know that there is no behavior they can be involved in that the parent will not forgive them for. Two years ago a man was found to be unfaithful to his wife. I was very disappointed in his behavior and in the way he was handling it. In my frustration I was very verbal about my disgust toward this man and spoke about my feelings in front of my children. My responses were extremely unforgiving, even though the man's acts of infidelity had no impact on me personally. It finally occurred to me that I was making a very poor statement to my children. As they listened to their father, they could surmise that perhaps there were certain behaviors that their dad did not forgive. Unless I corrected my attitude, my children could have been left with the thought that if they were ever involved in sexual sin they would not be able to count on Dad's love to help them. He is not very forgiving in that particular area, they might think. Parents need to teach their children about forgiveness. That lesson will not come across, though, unless they see us actually demonstrate forgiveness. It cannot be done unless we have a system in the home that does not put parent and child against each other. A disciplinary plan puts parent and child on the same team so that they can forgive.

A disciplinary plan teaches the child about the concept of forgiveness and then allows the child to know *he* is forgiven. This will make it that much easier for the child to understand what it means to be forgiven by God. The Lord's disciplinary plan is very organized. We, too, have been told ahead of time about the boundaries. Our nature is such, however, that we are unable to maintain the necessary behavior. The consequence was so great that our Parent decided to take the consequence upon Himself. Because of His sacrifice, we are able to receive forgiveness. Parents will not want to hinder their children from understanding that concept.

Discipline for the Sake of Your Apprentice

There is one final significant reason for a disciplinary plan in the home. We have seen how parents can help their children immensely as they grow up if a plan is consistently handled. It has also been established that this plan will give them the tools to develop as they enter the adult world. And as just discussed, a properly handled disciplinary plan will make it easier for the children to understand God and the forgiveness He offers. Now we come to one final reason why an easily understandable disciplinary plan is so important for children today. That reason is the children of tomorrow.

I am convinced that the reason many of us have struggled with this job of parenting and discipline is that our own parents did not know how to do it. Today's parents and grandparents grew up away from the farm and the extended family. Many of our parents did not have family help when they raised us. To add to that confusion, our childhood was a time when our parents were told that discipline was not necessary. They didn't recover from that fallacy until we were raised. In short, many of us did not grow up under a system of consistent discipline.

In years past, many young people spent time under a training system called an apprenticeship. A young person would watch a master and learn how a specific trade was done. Eventually that young person would grow up and perform the task himself. Today's parent is the craftsman who is training the next generation of parents. Our children are today's apprentices learning how to be tomorrow's parents and adults. Are they having the opportunity to learn how to set up a plan in the home that will allow for healthy growth for our grandchildren? Fifty years from now, will today's parent be happy with the parenting job that is taking place with the grandchildren? The parents of the next generation are being raised right now. Are we showing them how to do it properly? I hope so, since so much depends on it.

Parents must go to the effort of creating the "crust"—the plan—that holds the family together. Homes need a disciplinary plan so that the family members can have fun and enjoy each other's company. Loving the children isn't enough. Parents must like their children enough to want to set the boundaries that the family can play in. As parents, we cannot afford to fail in this. As the old adage says, by failing to plan we will be planning to fail, and the cost of that failure is too great. What we do today might just affect the generations to come.

Summary

1. A disciplinary plan provides the child and parent with a job description.

2. A disciplinary plan, handled consistently, teaches the child how to pursue excellence.

3. A disciplinary plan, handled properly, allows children to feel forgiven.

4. Parents who use a disciplinary plan in their home will raise a child who can reach his full potential when he's an adult.

5. Children who grow up in homes where there is a loving, consistent disciplinary plan will feel loved and will understand how to love their own children.

APPENDIX A

At parenting staff meetings it is often helpful to have a worksheet for evaluating a child's behavior and deciding how to best help the child. Often this can take some of the emotion out of the disciplinary planning. The following example of a worksheet can be used as is or rearranged to meet your own personal needs.

DISCIPLINARY PLAN WORKSHEET

Date: _____

Child: _____

Behavior in Question: _____

Questions to ask yourself:

1. Is this behavior rebellious or simply childish?

2. Is this behavior something that could carry over into adulthood? Will it have a lasting impact?

3. Is this behavior taking place because we do not have a consistent plan for correcting it?

4. Are we consistently using this plan?

5. Is the plan such that it is easily understandable?

6. Are we personally disciplined in this area? Are we setting a good example?

7. Is this a behavior that we are able to correct, or are we trying to control something that we cannot control?

New plan for correction of the behavior:

1. State the reason for the new plan to the child, and set a date to begin implementing it.

   That can be done on: _____ (date, time & location)

   It will be done by: _____ (ideally both parents)

2. Explain the new plan to be implemented to deal with this behavior during the talk with the child.

3. Explain the consequence for not living up to this responsibility.

4. The benefits of living up to this responsibility will be _____.

The adequacy or inadequacy of this plan will be reviewed by the parents: _____ (Make a date now.)

APPENDIX B

FOR FURTHER READING

Chapter 2

Dobson, James. *Dare to Discipline*. Wheaton, IL: Tyndale, 1970.

Richards, Lawrence O. *The Word Parents Handbook*. Waco, TX: Word, 1983.

Narramore, Bruce. *Help I'm a Parent*. Grand Rapids, MI: Zondervan, 1972.

Highlander, Don H. *Positive Parenting*. Waco, TX: Word, 1980.

Chapter 3

Brandt, Henry and Phil Landrum. *I Want to Enjoy My Children*. Grand Rapids, MI: Zondervan, 1975.

Chapter 4

Swets, Paul W. *How to Talk So Your Teen-Ager Will Listen*. Dallas, TX: Word, 1988.

Chapter 5

Stanley, Charles. *How to Keep Your Kids on Your Team*. Nashville, TN: Oliver Nelson, 1986.

Chapter 6

Barnes, Robert G. *Confident Kids*. Wheaton, IL: Tyndale, 1987.

Briggs, Dorothy Corkille. *Your Child's Self-Esteem*. Garden City, NY: Doubleday & Co., 1970.

Chapter 7

MacDonald, Gordon. *The Effective Father*. Wheaton, IL: Tyndale, 1985.

Chafin, Kenneth. *Is There a Family in the House?* Waco, TX: Word, 1978.

Hansel, Tim. *What Kids Need Most in a Dad*. Old Tappan, NJ: Revell, 1984.

Chapter 8

Swindoll, Charles. *Growing Wise in Family Life*. Portland, OR: Multnomah Press, 1988.

Chapter 10

Ackerman, Paul & Murry Kappelman. *Signals: What Is Your Child Really Telling You?* New York: Dial Press, 1978.

Chapter 11

Dobson, James. *Dare to Discipline*. Wheaton, IL: Tyndale, 1970.
Hendricks, Howard G. *Heaven Help the Home*. Wheaton, IL: Victor Books, 1978.

Chapter 13

Kesler, Jay. *Too Big to Spank*. Ventura, CA: Regal Books, 1978.

Chapter 14

Moore, Raymond & Dorothy. *Home Spun Schools*. Waco, TX: Word, 1982.

Chapter 15

Adams, Marjorie E. (Editor). *God in the Classroom*. Westchester, IL: Good News, 1970.
Joy, Donald M. *Bonding*. Waco, TX: Word, 1985.

Chapter 16

Bence, Evelyn. *Leaving Home*. Wheaton, IL: Tyndale, 1986.

Chapter 17

Garrison, Jayne. *The Christian Working Mother's Handbook*. Wheaton, IL: Tyndale, 1986.

Chapter 19

Faber, Adele and Elaine Mazlish. *Siblings Without Rivalry*. New York: Norton, 1987.

Chapter 21

Blue, Ron and Judy. *Money Matters for Parents*. Nashville, TN: Oliver Nelson, 1988.

Chapter 23

White, Joe. *Looking for Love in All the Wrong Places.* Wheaton, IL: Tyndale, 1983.

McDowell, Josh. *How to Help Your Child Say "NO."* Waco, TX: Word, 1987.

Chapter 24

Mains, Karen Burton. *Making Sunday Special.* Waco, TX: Word, 1987.

Murray, Andrew. *How to Raise Your Child for Christ.* Minneapolis, MN: Bethany House, 1975.

Sandford, John and Paula. *Restoring the Christian Family.* Plainfield, NJ: Logos, 1979.

Lewis, Paul. *40 Ways to Teach Your Child Values.* Wheaton, IL: Tyndale, 1985.

Elder, Carl A. *Values and Moral Development in Children.* Nashville, TN: Broadman Press, 1976.

Chapter 25

Barnes, Robert G. *Single Parenting: A Wilderness Journey.* Wheaton, IL: Tyndale, 1985.

Barnes, Robert G. *Single Parent Survival Guide.* Wheaton, IL: Tyndale, 1987.

Chapter 26

Houmes, Dan. *Growing in Step.* Richardson, TX: Today, 1985.

Chapter 27

Hansel, Tim. *When I Relax I Feel Guilty.* Elgin, IL: David C. Cook, 1979.

Chapter 28

Dobson, James. *Love Must Be Tough.* Waco, TX: Word, 1983.

Dobson, James. *The Strong Willed Child.* Wheaton, IL: Tyndale, 1978.

Kennedy, D. James. *Your Prodigal Child.* Nashville, TN: Nelson, 1988.

Stewart, Mark A. and Sally Wendkos Olds. *Raising a Hyperactive Child.* New York: Harper & Row, 1973.

Chapter 29

Barnes, Robert G. *Confident Kids.* Wheaton, IL: Tyndale, 1987.

We want to hear from you. Please send your comments about this book to us in care of the address below. Thank you.

ZONDERVAN™

GRAND RAPIDS, MICHIGAN 49530 USA

WWW.ZONDERVAN.COM